# From Iowa Cornfields to Fernwood

## *My Life and Stories*

By Francis E. Stewart, Sr.

Published in the United States of America

By Francis Elon Stewart, Sr.

Copyright © 2011, Francis Elon Stewart, Sr.

All Rights Reserved.

No part of this publication may be reproduced, stored in a retrieval system, or transmitted in any form or by any means, without the prior permission, in writing, of the publisher and author.

First published by Francis Elon Stewart, Sr. June 2011

ISBN-13: 978-0615497686

ISBN-10: 0615497683

Printed in the United States of America

This book is printed on acid-free paper.

For Clarice, my dear wife and helpmate.
Without her I could not have been a whole person.
Her agape love has uplifted and sustained me.

For our children Frank, Donna, and Susan
and our grandchildren Jeanne and Corinne.

# Millennium Letter to the Editor

## Pickens County Progress

Dear Editor,

In no time at all, or so it seems, this century is drawing to a close. Yet, many events of the century linger in my memory.

As a young boy, seeing and having my picture taken watching Charles Lindberg, "The Lone Eagle," climbing into his plane, surrounded by soldiers as he continued his barn storming travel across the USA following his historic flight to Paris.

Walking three-quarters of a mile to a one-room schoolhouse fall, winter, and spring. Enjoying the cherry red hot pot-bellied stove in the middle of the schoolroom on cold winter days and helping milk twelve cows on cold winter nights.

Moving from the frozen North to the sunny South during the Great Depression, traveling on a school bus from Olive Springs in Cobb County to Piedmont Park and we kids lined up on each side of the road all through the park as Franklin D. Roosevelt passed through in his open-top car. I have often wondered if the sight of all those World War I baby boomers led to his famous "ill-fed, ill-clothed" speech.

Finishing high school at Acworth in 1940, attending the University of Georgia on a partial 4-H scholarship, selling Bibles in North Carolina in the summer of 1941, taking my very first airplane ride at Athens with my roommate on December 7th, 1941. Upon landing the plane, we were surprised to find no one near the planes and everyone huddled around the radio. Pearl Harbor had been bombed and we knew we would soon be at WAR.

Enlisting in the Army Air Force after serving with the Civil Aeronautics Administration as a radio and teletype operator in Vero Beach, Tampa, and Atlanta. Following training at Keesler Field, Missouri, Sioux Falls, South Dakota, Yuma, Arizona, and Goldsburg, North Carolina, I was shipped overseas to Italy and assigned to the B-25 outfit in the 12th Air Force as a radio operator and gunner. Witnessing some of the human misery of war near Naples, Italy, as children and adults fought for the garbage thrown out by the military. Seeing a small lad on an outside ledge window of the Allied Transient Mess and begging for bread. My loaf not delivered to the lad as a large girl jumped and snatched it from my uplifted hand and looking back, witnessing the sad look on the boy's face.

Attending Mercer University after the war and getting both a liberal arts education and finding my life's greatest treasure – my future bride and now my dear wife of more than half a century.

Attending a conference at Princeton University and, while walking across the campus, met the famous man wearing his traditional sweatshirt and baggy pants. None other than Albert Einstein.

Attending Crozer Seminary for two years with Martin Luther King, Jr., only he was simply M. L. or Mike then. We all thought the name Martin Luther was pretty heavy baggage to hang on a young black student from Atlanta, GA. We were to learn different in a few years, and thankfully, I still have some of the letters I received from my friend Martin Luther King, Jr.

Serving as pastor of a small middle Georgia Baptist church and getting to know and love some of God's finest folks. Serving in Georgia state government with Bill Burson and later, in the Governor's Office of Planning and Budget under Jimmy Carter, George Busbee, and Joe Frank Harris.

Now we are in the jet age, computers, and preparing to leap into the next century. Someone said, "The past is prologue." William Faulkner said something like, "The past is not yet passed."

Just a final thought. There are a lot of us around these parts who have lived through most of this century. If you are interested in history, take the time to talk with some of the old-timers here in Pickens County. They will surely let you know how far we have come and perhaps make you think about how far we have yet to go.

Best wishes to all in the year 2000 and may God bless you.

Sincerely,

Francis E. Stewart

December 30, 1999

# Contents

Millennium Letter to the Editor    v

Iowa Years    1

    Accidents    9
    The Dust Bowl    10
    Chickens    10
    Milking Cows    10
    Iowa Christmas    13

My Early Schooling    15

    Lake Center School    18
    Freeman Township School    19

Luther Samuel Stewart    21

Grace Minta Pritchard Stewart    29

The Great Transition    33

    Battlefield Camp    38
    Olive Springs School    40

The Store    43

    Sales Vendors    45
    The Regulars    46
    The CCC Boys    51
    Kennesaw School    51
    Acworth High School    53

# Contents

New York World's Fair  **57**

University of Georgia  **59**

Selling Bibles in North Carolina  **65**

Vero Beach, Tampa, and Atlanta  **73**

War  **79**

Mercer  **93**

Gibbs Memorial Baptist Church  **99**

Crozer Seminary  **101**

    Inter-Seminary Conferences  **104**
    Father Divine's Heaven  **104**
    Martin Luther King, Jr.  **106**

Monticello  **115**

    Clarice  **126**
    Our Young Family  **128**
    Our Kids Tell All – (Notes from Journal, 1952 - 1963)  **129**
    Kathy  **133**

Milledgeville  **135**

War on Poverty  **141**

    Salisbury-Rowan County Community Service Council  **141**
    Iredell County Action Research and Evaluation  **142**
    Atlanta 1968, State Office of Economic Opportunity  **146**
    Family Memories of Statesville  **148**

# Contents

Prayer in the Midst of Change **151**

Hedonists **152**

Four Governors **153**

    Lester Maddox (Governor 1967 – 1971) **153**
    Jimmy Carter (Governor, 1971 – 1975) **155**
    George Busbee (Governor 1975 – 1983) **160**
    Joe Frank Harris (Governor 1983 – 1991) **164**
    Flight Through a Hail Storm **165**
    Make Your Voice Heard By Government **165**

Desert Flowers **167**

Fernwood **175**

Prayer of Gratitude and Hope **185**

Benediction **186**

Acknowledgements **187**

# Iowa Years

## 1923 - 1934

My earliest memories of our Iowa years, probably from around 1927, are focused on farm life. At that time, we were the Stone family. Jack Stone, Grace Pritchard Stone, me, and my two younger sisters, Dorothy and Barbara. Many years later, our last name would change.

At that time we lived as sharecroppers on the Brady place. Where we lived was always called a place, never called a home, as we were only tenant sharecroppers. Rent was paid to the landlord with a portion of the corn and oats that were harvested.

All of us had farm work and chores. Chores consisted of feeding horses, cows, pigs and chickens, gathering eggs, milking the cows, separating the cream from the whole milk, feeding the skim milk to the hogs, and cleaning out the horse stalls, cow barn, pig pens, and chicken houses.

Francis and Dorothy at the Brady place, 1928

John Pritchard (Grandfather of Grace Pritchard Stone), Barbara, and Francis, 1928. Great-grandfather John Pritchard was a Civil War veteran.

Around the age of four, I received my first chore that I can remember. Dad assigned me the task of breaking ear corn in half and putting it in a metal bushel basket. This was for feeding the horses at noon. I started early, and was diligent but not strong enough to break the ears in half, even though I repeatedly banged them on the side of the metal basket. When Dad came in from the field at noon, he helped me finish.

Another early task I had was getting the mail from the mailbox. The mailbox was a good half mile away. I was not yet able to read but managed to roll a wooden keg home. However, it belonged to Ed O'Neal and not to us. Mother said I defended my action by stating, "Well it says "says" on it." "Says" was my word for "words." I was learning how to read and was excited to find something with words on it.

I don't know how old I was when I was given my first "opportunity" to milk cows. I was assigned the oldest and most gentle cow to milk. After I had milked a bit, Dad came to check on me and asked what I was doing. I told him that I was pulling the slivers out of the cow's teats. He said those are not slivers but warts that looked like wooden slivers. The cow had not kicked me and endured my amateur surgery.

Milking cows was a morning and night chore 365 days a year, so we were never far from home, summer or winter. Once or twice, we did have someone to come in and do the milking when we made a trip to Minnesota. Milking on a winter night was a real task. Frequently we had to put on heavy clothes and overshoes and carry milk pails and a lantern to the barn. Then we would take off some of the clothes, as the barn was warm from the heat from the cows. Also, sitting on a one-leg stool with a pail between the knees and pulling and squeezing a cow's teats was good exercise. Especially as the pail began to fill up. We would have to squeeze our knees harder to keep the pail of milk from spilling.

I don't think I was ever kicked by a cow, although by the time I was eleven years old I was milking four of the twelve cows. Dorothy also did her share of milking and has a full share of milking stories to tell. When we moved to Georgia and as boys challenged one another, I found that I had by far the strongest grip in my age group. This was thanks to years of squeezing cow's teats.

Cleaning out the gutters in the cow barns was a fairly regular and demanding task. The manure was shoveled out the door into a pile where it remained frozen in winter, and then hauled out in the spring and spread across the fields with a manure spreader.

Springtime was planting time. That was Dad's job. Oat seed was broadcast from a planter attached to the back of the wagon. The gadget spun and caused the seed to be spread over a fairly large area.

Corn planting was a different challenge. At that time, corn was planted in checkerboard squares. A roll of corn planting wire was stretched across the length of the field. This wire had little knots at about three-foot lengths. As the planter hit each knot along the wire, it tripped the planter and allowed a few grains of corn seed to be dropped. The purpose of this kind of planting was to allow plowing both lengthwise and crosswise in the field. It must have been a real challenge to stretch the wire and make the wire knots parallel with each row planted. I am sure other farmers looked at each field of corn as they passed by to see if indeed the farmer was matching his rows of corn so as to allow good cross cultivation. This planting practice has long since been abandoned.

One of the tasks related to field work that was assigned to Dorothy and me and probably Barbara, was to take water out to Dad in the field. It was carried in a quart jar. If we were late, Dad would yell from the field for us to bring him water. He never, so far as I can remember, carried water to the field. Maybe he just wanted some company for a few minutes.

Dorothy, Francis, and Barbara, around 1930

Springtime was also a time of adventure for us. Fish were running up the creeks, streams, and even tile ditches to spawn. Farmers usually knew when they were running before the game wardens. The farmers usually had spears that looked like several large fish hooks only turned straight and attached to a pole. Then it was an easy task to stand along the creek, or near a bridge and spear the pike and pickerel as they made their way upstream from the lakes.

Once Dad got his share to bring home and reported his good fortune to our neighbor Fred Broadie. Fred and his hired man went out and got their share, only to be caught by an alert game warden. Fred had his fishing equipment taken away and had to pay a fine. I am sure that most farmers, including Uncle Iver Oppedal always got their share of fish in the spring, but were alert enough to keep from being spotted by the game warden.

Dorothy and I once made quite a catch in our neighbor's pasture. The carp were coming up the tile ditches and attempting to spawn in a small drainage pond. However, most of the water had drained back into the lake and left only about a dozen carp in the very small pond. We managed to catch all of them and carried them home. They were good-sized fish, probably each weighing three to four pounds or more. Nobody ate carp, so far as I know, and I guess they were tossed out for the hogs to eat. But Dorothy and I remember that as probably our biggest catch.

Francis and Dorothy Stone; Russell, Richard, and Earl Sampson. 1927

Another memorable fishing experience happened when we lived on the Courtright place. The whole family went down to nearby Trumbull Lake to fish for bullheads (called catfish in the South). The fish were biting as fast as we could bait the hooks and pull them in. Mother left her line with no bait in the edge of the lake while she looked after my baby brother Dallas. The next thing she noticed was her pole going out into the lake. She ran into the water, grabbed the pole and pulled in the fish. I don't know how many fish we caught that afternoon, but like the Bible story, we had baskets full.

Summertime and late spring were times for picnics in the state park and Memorial Day (Decoration Day in Iowa) at the Crown Hill cemetery. When the American Legion men fired their rifles and played taps and the echo finished sounding, we boys dived to collect as many spent rifle cartridges as we could stuff in our pockets. Picnics at Lost Island State Park usually brought out all of our relatives plus most of the farm families in the area around Ruthven. The lake shore was not a sand beach but a rocky and boulder-strewn shore. Still we could go swimming if we wished. I don't remember swimming, but I do remember getting leeches on my legs a time or two from being in the lake. We were surrounded by lakes: Lost Island, Trumbull, Mud Lake, Round Lake and even Dan Green Slough. In fact much of this area of northwest Iowa had to be tiled in for drainage in order to be farmed.

Late summer was oat shocking and thrashing time. Shocking oats was a job done in hot summer weather. I remember working with our hired man when I was about ten or eleven shocking oats. The oats were in bundles and tied with binder twine. Our job was to follow the oat binder, pick up the bundles, stack five, six, or more bundles with the heads upright and then cap the stack with one or two more bundles. It was a hot job and, hopefully, shocking and thrashing could be completed before rains came. Anyway, I remember shocking oats because Dad paid me the sum total of fifty cents for my work that summer shocking oats. Remember, this was in the early 1930s during the Great Depression, although as kids we were never aware of any depression because we were no different from everyone else we knew on Iowa farms.

Thrashing was another matter. It required teams of horses with wagons to catch the oats as they poured out from the thrashing machine. More teams of horses with hay racks went to the field and we used pitch forks to pick up the bundles from the shocks and pitch them into the hay racks. Some workers tended the tractor and thrashing machine and still others worked the straw.

The straw was blown into the barn and used for winter bedding for the livestock or blown out onto a big pile to be food for animals in hard winters, if the animals wanted it, and most did. One of my jobs was to work in the barn and help spread the straw as it was blown in, another hot dusty job. We also put up hay for the livestock and I don't remember how the hay was separated from the straw in the barn. We also had a straw pile on the Courtright place, but not on the Tripp place. These were two other farms where we sharecropped in Iowa.

Fall was corn-picking time and plowing time. I never had to work the horses. The only time I remember being asked to help with the horses was once, when Dad asked me to hold the lines while he tended to something else. Naturally, I got tired of holding the lines and tried a simpler way. I wrapped the lines over my neck. Dad was horrified when he returned and spotted me with the lines around my neck. If the horses had bolted away, that would have been the end of me.

It was always fascinating to watch the plow turn the ground and see all of the earth worms turned up. It was also feast time for the gulls as they flocked in by the dozens and hundreds to gobble up the worms.

Corn picking was another difficult part of farm work in the 1920s and early 1930s. I remember going out with Mother and Dad and staying in the wagon as they picked the corn. The wagon had bang boards on one side so that the pickers could simply break off an ear from the stalk and without looking up toss the ears against the bang-boards and let them fall into the wagon. Pickers had a metal hook attached to one hand that was used to pull off most of the shuck, then they broke off the ear from the stalk and tossed in into the wagon. It was a hard job as once the wagon was full, it had to be hauled into the corn crib and the corn shoveled into the crib. We did not have mechanical equipment such as elevators to move the corn from the wagon into the crib, but other farmers did.

Picking corn was also a race against the oncoming winter. If the rains came too early, it was impossible to get into the field. If the snows came too early, it might be necessary for some farmers to wait until spring to finish the fall harvest. Then too, during the Great Depression corn was selling for only cents a bushel. For a while, we burned corn in the stove for fuel. However, it worked better if we used some coal with the corn.

During harsh winters, the pheasants would make their way up to the corn cribs and I doubt if many farmers ever tried to shoot them, as they too were in survival mode.

Farm children learned about sex education without ever knowing what it was called. Farmers with milk cows had to have a bull, and brood mares had to be serviced by a good stud. Most farmers did not keep a stud but could easily hire one as needed. We not only had laying hens, but also had an incubator and brooder for hatching fertile eggs and growing baby chicks. So, we had to have an adequate supply of roosters.

Winter months were long, but we were so attuned to the seasons and too young to pay them much attention. Dorothy and I received a pair of ice skates one Christmas when we lived on the Tripp place. We could hardly wait to get on the frozen lake. We quickly learned to skate and turned our coats up and used them as sails as we skated across the lake.

Sleds were of little use to us as the ground was usually too level for sledding. However, there were times when we were allowed to tie the sleds behind the car and be towed. Sleds were also used for transporting us to Lake Center School one winter.

One extremely harsh winter when we lived on the Tripp place and we had a lot of snow on the ground, the snow plow had a hard time clearing the road. Later the temperature dropped far below zero. We did not own a thermometer and as the wind was almost calm, we were sent to school. We had to walk almost a mile to the Freeman Township school. When we got there, our cheeks were frozen. Dorothy says that Barbara and I were behind and in serious trouble. The teacher and Harold Roland were at the school but no other kids bothered to come, or their parents had thermometers and had too much sense to send their kids that day. The temperature was -28° Fahrenheit. Harold Roland then brought us home in his car.

The snows were not all bad. The air is fairly warm under the snow and snow houses are fun to play in. We did make many tunnels in the snow drifts. Also one of our favorite winter games at school was Fox and Geese. We tread out a big wheel, made the spokes, and used the hub as safety zone. One person was the fox and the rest were geese. The fox could catch you anytime you were out of the hub. Once caught, you became the fox until you were able to catch another goose.

Of course, we did our share of foolish things too. As very young children on the Brady place, Dorothy and I took a box of matches from the kitchen and slipped out near the barn. We then found a piece of iron and tried to burn it. We lit most of the matches and then hid the burned matches under a rock or brick. I suppose we then returned the remainder of the matches to the kitchen. Later Dad accidentally kicked over the frozen brick or rock and discovered the burned match stubs. He became very irate and upset, not simply because we had taken the matches but also because we had elected to hide under the gasoline barrel beside the barn to strike our matches.

Another time, Dorothy became enamoured with the frost on the windmill. She proceeded to lick the frost with her tongue only to find her tongue frozen solid to the metal. She lost some skin and did not try that again.

About that same time, I caught hell for what I did with the girls' dolls. They said they were through with them and I asked if I could take them apart and see what was inside the dolls that made them cry. They said OK. But after I took the squeakers out, the girls changed their minds. They started to cry and reported to mother what I had done. Mother was very angry over what I had done to the expensive toys and I received a whipping.

I thought the girls were finished with them as I had found them in a snow bank. But children frequently leave their toys in one place, forget where they left them, and turn to some other toy.

## Accidents

Children living on farms are exposed to many opportunities to get hurt. Dorothy was run over by a grain wagon during thrashing season. I don't know if it was empty or loaded. Everybody was busy. The women were all busy preparing the big meal at noon. We kids were pretty much on our own and it was a time of excitement for us. Anyway, Dorothy was not taken to the hospital for x-rays. In fact, I think the nearest hospital was many miles away. I doubt if she was taken to the doctor, but to this day, she thinks some of her back problems may stem from being run over by a wagon as a young child.

As a toddler, my brother Dallas received a bad scar while playing in the house near the washing machine. This was when we lived on the Tripp place and Dallas was probably just learning to walk. He got some lye on his ankle and it left a permanent scar. Mother may have been using the lye to make soap.

Barbara, Dorothy, and I were playing with an old cider press that had been left there by the owner or a prior tenant. Dorothy and I were turning it and Barbara got her finger caught in the cogs. She still has a scar on her finger.

I don't remember any serious accidents that happened to me. Once I was attempting to catch some pigeons in the barn loft. The barn was nearly full of hay or straw and I could reach the top of the barn. In chasing the pigeons, one flew into a window breaking it. Part of the glass fell and hit my hand just below the left thumb and left a permanent scar.

Also I was once hit in the head with a baseball bat while playing a made-up game at Freeman Township school. The Zealstra boys had brought big tires to school that we rolled around. The game was for one of us to roll past the guy with the bat. The boy with the bat swung the bat attempting to knock down the tire, only he missed the tire and hit me in the head. Some who read this may say, "Now I know why Francis always seemed a bit daffy."

I guess we also had our share of childhood diseases, but none stands out in my memory.

## The Dust Bowl

The Great Depression was also the time of the dust storms across the Great Plains. Farm land to the west of Iowa had been turned into vast wheat fields. With the long dry periods and the winds across the great plains, clouds of dust swept across the states. I well remember dust drifting against farm fences between the Courtright place and the Prichard farm. The drifts were the same as the snowdrifts of winter, except they were black. I am sure that was one of the many reasons Dad decided it was about time to return to his native Georgia.

## Chickens

Catching chickens before the late fall or early fall Iowa freeze was always a problem. Chickens roosted in the trees during the warm summer months and continued this practice on into the fall.

We had to go out after dark and climb trees or use long poles with wire hooks at the end to hook the sleeping birds by the foot. Usually it would take more than one night and those we missed had a frozen comb that turned black or dropped off.

Keeping chickens in the chicken house for several months was not so pleasant either. Cleaning out a chicken house in the spring was absolutely the worst job of all. The roosting racks had to be cleaned off and all the droppings under the roost had to be taken out.

I don't recall much about cleaning hog barns but I did clean out the horse barns and cow barns on many occasions. I will take cleaning a cow or horse barn over a chicken house any time.

## Milking Cows

The cows had to be milked twice a day, seven days a week. Cows were not milked at any old time, but milked 12 hours apart. (By 1999, some high-yielding cows were milked three or more times a day.) Therefore, much of our time revolved around cow milking time. In the late spring, summer, and possibly early fall on the Tripp place, the cows were driven a half mile to the pasture after milking and then back in the afternoon.

Some ground feed was placed in their feed bins and hay in winter. Each cow seemed always to know her own stall. Old Beck, the largest and strongest and best milker, was always at the head of the line waiting to come into the barn and be milked. One quickly learned to step aside as the doors were opened because the cows would run to their stalls.

Once in their stalls, their heads were locked into the stanchions, otherwise some cows would back out as soon as their feed was eaten and attempt to get another cow's feed, or back out before milking was completed. At any event, we had twelve cows to milk and some had to wait their turn. I had four to milk in 1934, and I don't know how many Dorothy and my mother Grace had to milk.

Dad usually milked the cows that were the most temperamental, those that would kick and knock you into the gutter if they were so minded. Dorothy and I were assigned the most gentle cows. Dad had some shackles that he put on the temperamental cows. There were plenty of times when he cussed, kicked and beat ornery cows. Dad was no gentle Quaker when it came to milking cows.

We sat on a one-legged wooden stool and held the milk bucket between our legs. Milk would come very slowly at first, unless the cow was fresh and full of milk and then the milk would be streaming out as soon as she got in the stanchion. I don't know if we squeezed the front or hind teats first, I suppose we took those that were largest and seemed to hold the most milk. Anyway, milk quickly made a pinging sound as the streams of warm milk hit the bottom of the bucket.

The cats were always around during milking time and expected us to squirt a few streams into their mouths which we usually did. In fact, if Dad was not watching, Dorothy and I might squirt a short burst of milk at each other. In wintertime steam seemed to come from our breaths, the cows breaths, and the warm milk. Quickly the rhythmic sounds of milk going in the buckets changed as the buckets began to fill. A nearly full bucket of milk was quite heavy and, if you were not careful, the bucket could slip from between your legs and spill.

I suppose some folks sat the buckets on the barn floor, but our cow barns were not very clean and milk had to be poured into five-gallon cans until run through the separator. After all the cows were milked, the stanchions were unlocked and the cows turned out of the barn, unless it was down below zero. In that case, the cows were given extra hay and kept in the barn.

Milk had to be separated in the hand-cranked separator. Cream came out one spout and into a ten-gallon container and skim milk went into another. Skim milk was then mixed with feed and fed to the hogs. The mixing was done in a big, steel barrel then dipped and poured into the hog troughs. Again, one had to be careful as the hogs climbed on top of one another in their haste to get the slop, as we called the mix.

Young calves also were given milk and taught to drink from a bucket. I believe the trick was to let the calf suck on one's finger then lower the finger into the bucket and suddenly the calf was drinking from the bucket. However, the calves would instinctively butt their heads up as they do when getting milk from the cow. If you were not alert, the calf would knock the bucket from your hands and spill the milk.

The cream was cooled in a water tank and kept there until taken to the creamery. Of course, in the dead of winter this was not necessary. It could be stored in an out room of the house. After the milk was run through, the separator was flushed with warm water each night. At least once a day the key parts had to be taken to the house and washed. I am sure that was always another of Mother's tasks.

Cleaning out a cow barn was a necessary task. In wintertime, the manure could freeze and would be most difficult to handle. The manure pile was always close to the barn, and was a sloppy mess in wet weather and during spring thawing. When weather was suitable, the manure was forked or shoveled into a manure spreader and hauled off and spread across a field, where the next crop of corn or oats was to be planted. I think we spent at least three to four hours a day in and around the barn.

At the creamery some of the cream could be swapped for Land-O-Lakes butter or cheese. I do not know how much the cream check amounted to, as I never saw one or heard how much it amounted to. We always had Holstein cows that gave a lot of milk, but their milk was not as rich in butterfat as the milk of Jersey or Guernsey cows.

In the dead of winter, morning and evening milking had to be done in the dark. Kerosene lanterns, and later one gas mantle lantern, were used for light. Here was an added danger. If a lantern was dropped or knocked over it could easily set the barn on fire. Somehow we always managed in the dark, dimly-lit barns.

I suppose there have been books written on this subject, but this is what I remember about milking on a northwest Iowa farm in the early 1930s. I am sure that way of tending a dairy farm is rather primitive compared to today's mechanical milking process, hauling, and barn cleaning operations.

## Iowa Christmas

Compared to today's Christmas season, Christmas on the farms in Iowa during the late 1920s and early 1930s was vastly different. I do not remember having a Christmas tree, as evergreen trees were uncommon around farm houses and if they were available, they were used as windbreaks located on the north and west sides of the house.

Mother would string popcorn as a decoration. Where we hung our stockings I do not remember, as we did not have a fireplace. On Christmas morning, we found apples, oranges, nuts, and hard candy in our stockings. Usually we could expect to find some new clothes. Winter coats were a must. Overshoes, also, were a must for the snow, mud, and slush from melting snow.

The big event would be Christmas at Grandmother's Pritchard's home. There were plenty of mashed potatoes and gravy and canned vegetables from the summer garden would be brought out. There would be fresh meat from a winter kill of a hog or a calf. Also, we had plenty of chicken to eat. Rich, whipped cream was served on puddings, cake, or ice cream. Children usually ate at a separate table. I do not remember what age we were when we were allowed to eat at the table with the big folks.

Some kind of preparations for Christmas also would be made at the school house. I suppose there were decorations made from coloring and paper cutouts.

A sled or ice skates were the very best Christmas presents a boy or girl could expect, and Dorothy and I did receive these presents one year.

Dorothy has also reminded us numerous times that she once hung her stocking several weeks after Christmas to see if she would have another harvest of goodies. However, the next morning she found her sock filled with coal, rocks, and sticks.

# My Early Schooling

Before we started to public school, Mother would read to Dorothy, Barbara, and I at night after chores and supper and just before bedtime. She read Bible stories, *Huckleberry Finn*, *The Adventures of Tom Sawyer*, and other books. Mother read to us by a kerosene lamp and later by an Alladin lamp, as there was no electricity on Iowa farms in the 1920s. I believe she obtained the books by mail from a state lending library.

Mother would read a few chapters each night and we would have to wait for the next night's reading to learn what happened next. In our minds' imaginations we could feel the danger Tom and Becky felt when they were lost in the cave and threatened by Injun Joe. Mother would get caught up in the stories too. She would laugh when Huck and Tom decided to free their slave friend. Even if they had to "rot and go to hell."

Francis (circled) watches Charles Lindbergh on a barnstorming tour in Sioux City, Iowa, after Lindbergh's historic flight over the Atlantic. Another opportunity for learning.

## My Early Schooling

So, my love of books and reading was taught and caught in those very early pre-school years. Before I was five, Mother decided that I was ready for the public school. Learning at Lake Center was a totally new and different experience and I remember very little about the first grade. My first grade memories of the classroom were unpleasant. Something that had to do with discipline, I suppose. The playground was a much more pleasant and memorable experience for me at Lake Center. There was lots of space and, as I recall, there were no teachers around to tell us what to play, how to play, or where to play.

At recess we could walk across the road to a filling station to buy candy and soft drinks, but I don't recall that any of us ever had any money to spend. Anyway. I was only five years old in the spring of 1928 and almost through the first grade.

My formal education was paralleled by what I was seeing, doing, and learning on the farm, first on the Brady place and later the Tripp and Courtright places. Farm work was very hard with lots and lots of manual labor, but at age five it was the only life we children knew. There were cows to milk, milk to separate into cream and skim milk, animals to be fed, eggs to be gathered, and the garden planted, weeded, and harvested. There were potato rows (lots and lots of potatoes) and potato bugs to be picked off and put in little jars of kerosene.

I watched Dad at work in the field, planting, plowing, harvesting, and we carried water to him in the field. I learned about seed time and harvest, spring, summer, fall, and winter. I learned something of our dependence on our animals and on the weather for the harvest.

Harvesting oats and thrashing oats required lots of help and neighbors took turns helping with thrashing. Thrashers ate well and so did we kids during this season.

My early years on an Iowa farm were an absorbing, educational experience that I have never forgotten. My practical farm education I remember far better than what I learned at Lake Center School or, later, at the one-room Freeman Township School.

Since I attended the little one-room Freeman Township School for four or five years, I have clearer and better memories of it. There were seven grades in one room.

The one-room Freeman Township School and playground covered about one acre of land. Again, I remember the playground better than the classroom. There were two outhouses, one for boys and the other for the girls, at opposite far corners of the school ground. For games, we had pop

## My Early Schooling

the whip and pump-pump-pull-away. In winter we played fox and geese in the snow. We made up games like rolling tires and batting them down with baseball bats.

One of my teachers, a fine lady, was a member of the Seventh Day Adventist Church. One weekend, she invited all of the boys in the school into her home to spend the night. I don't remember much about the occasion except that she and her parents were nice folks.

I suppose the girls were invited to her home to spend the night at another time. It was not difficult for her to provide this entertainment, as there were only about a dozen of us in the school.

Transportation to the Freeman Township School was easy; we walked in fall, winter, and spring. There was no school bus route since we lived slightly less than a mile from the school. In winter, we wore plenty of clothes, coats, stocking caps, mittens, and overshoes. We had an entry way in the school building to leave our coats and overshoes.

The situation was different at Lake Center School. We rode to school in some kind of wagon with flaps down the side. The wagon was pulled by horses. In winter with snow on the ground, we rode to school in a sled pulled by a team of horses. The sled had lots of straw in the bottom for added insulation.

Once in the month of February, I was taking Felix the Cat valentines to school for my classmates. The sled was moving very slowly as we passed near Barney Sampson's home and we kids jumped out and ran behind the sled for a few yards. Unfortunately, all of my valentines fell into the snow and I was unable to give out my valentines. However, the valentines were recovered by a friend and returned to me. I gave out my valentines one day late, but this was a sad event that I have not forgotten.

Usually we received new shoes in the fall and they were to last until the next spring. In the summer months we did not wear shoes. There were plenty of opportunities to stub our toes, step on a sharp rock, a tack, or a nail. Somehow, we survived all of that and had tough, thick soles on our feet by the time to get new shoes in the fall. Red Goose shoes were the favorite. Their motto was "Half the fun of having feet is Red Goose shoes." As I recall, they were usually bought at Hastings store where we traded eggs for groceries. Also, I think we received some kind of toy or trinket along with our new shoes, if they were Red Goose shoes.

I attended Lake Center School in the first grade, Freeman Township School in the second through fourth grades, and then back to Lake Center School for the fifth through seventh grades.

## Lake Center School

The Lake Center School was both the first and last school I attended in Iowa. It was a large, two-story brick school and vastly different from the one-room township schools in the area. Lake Center even had a Manual Training center with lots of tools that made an impression on me from the very first grade. I don't remember the teachers.

Mother sent me to school at a very young age. I was about four years and seven months old when she sent me to school. Because Mother had been a schoolteacher, I guess you would say in today's language I was home-schooled during my first four-plus years and also for many years after. She taught me to read and I remember the first words were, "Come and play with me today." So I suppose she decided I was ready for school, and besides, Mother had house chores, field work, and Dorothy and Barbara to look after.

During my very first days at school I was not a happy camper. About all I remember from those very early days was the teacher trying to pull me out of my seat. I had locked both arms around the top of the desk and refused to be moved. I remember more about the outside play area. Mother very early on asked me if I had met the school principal. I said yes and he had spoken to us. "What did he say?" Mother asked. I replied, "He said, 'You kids get off my car!'"

I also remember getting my very first Coca Cola at that school. We were supposed to collect five Coca Cola bottle caps to get a free Coke. However, everyone got a free Coke. I did not like it, though. It tasted horribly strong. It seems Coca Cola was marketed to the kids even way back in the 1920s.

During the end of the school year, one of my last years at Lake Center, the teacher was busy with the girls making something for year-end activities. We boys decided to play hookey and go to the creek about a half mile away. We had a nice outing and expected to be in some trouble when we returned. However, the teacher and the girls acted as if they had not even missed us. I suppose we were a bit disappointed at that.

My cousin Alan Oppedal, in his account of the Prichard and Capener families has a lot more to say about Lake Center School. Like Freeman Township School, it has long since disappeared. In fact, with the declining farm population in rural Iowa, many schools have been closed and merged with town schools or other schools.

The names of the students I remember from Freeman Township School are Ruth and Bobby Broadie; Harold, Dale, Ione, and Margaret Zielstrea;

# My Early Schooling

Anna Hanson; and Harry and Donald Dobbins. There were a few more, but those are the only names I remember. We were probably closer to the Dobbins boys than any of the others, and I know our parents were always close to the Dobbins families. Harry Dobbins had a bad scar on his face from having been burned as a child. They were friendly, caring boys.

In winter months, the teacher or parents sometimes brought a very big pot of soup to school. The soup was heated on top of the large stove and served to us at noon. Sometimes the big stove would be cherry red, but it did keep the one-room school warm.

During the early days of the Great Depression some of the farm families were given surplus food. They were called commodities. When some of the kids came to school and talked about their commodities as if it were Christmas time again, Dorothy came home and wanted to know why we were not getting commodities too.

I left Lake Center School when we moved to Georgia in 1934. I was eleven years old and in the seventh grade.

## Freeman Township School

Freeman Township School was about a mile from our home on the Tripp place. Most of the time we walked to school. We passed by the Broadie farm and usually walked with Bobby and Ruth Broadie. Once, while walking home I found a pipe wrench that had been unearthed from a recent pass of the road grader. I was carrying the wrench and somehow we got in a fight with Bobby and Ruth. There were three of us (me, Dorothy, and Barbara) and two of them, so we won. They ran home crying and told their mother. She came running out to the road and saw me carrying the pipe wrench and immediately thought I had slugged one of her children with the wrench. This I most certainly had not done. Needless to say, their mother was slow to let us play together again.

The Freeman Township School was a one-room school with a very large stove. The stove was not in the middle of the room but about two-thirds of the way to the front. Desks had ink wells, although I doubt if any of us ever used ink. Each grade would have a time to come up to the recitation bench, which was located directly in front of the teachers desk.

Spelling I remember. Ione Zielstra was my only classmate who was in my same grade. She was the better speller, so I would attempt to sit on the side of the bench where I would get the easiest words. I was smart enough to work through the list of words to be spelled, pick out the most difficult ones, and then attempt to get on the side of the bench where I was least likely to get the hard words. I knew the teacher went straight down the list and usually started with the student on her right. Thus, I assumed that I would be required to spell exactly half the words on the list. Therefore, I tried to be seated so as to get the easy half to spell.

The two teachers I remember were Bernadine Arney and Carrie Nelson. We did not have a well at the school and in the spring and fall someone, usually the older children, had to take a pail and walk about a fourth of a mile up the hill to a farmer's well. One day I told Miss Nelson I wanted to go with the older girl to get the water. I thought she said OK, and went for the water. At recess time, the teacher told me I had to stay in as I had disobeyed her. I said, no, she gave me permission, and proceeded to walk out. She grabbed me to keep me in the classroom and as I tried to pull away, I broke her wrist watch. At that point we both cried.

The outdoor toilets were at the far lower northwest and northeast corners of the school lot. On one of my very earliest days at the school, I kissed an older, pretty girl. I guess she was also one of the older boys' girlfriend. Anyway, several jumped me and I then found a club for a counter attack. The boys all ran into the boys toilet and braced themselves against the door. However, the door had a big crack in it and I used the club to come down hard and through the crack. It hit one of the boys on the arm, and then they came out and swarmed over me.

As a very young lad, I had only my younger sisters to play with and I was forbidden to hit or harm them. However, we took turns with the O'Neals hauling cream to the creamery in Ruthven. Bobby O'Neal would come with his mother and would jump out of the car and punch me. Then he would jump back in the car. Finally, Mother told me that if I did not punch Bobby back the next time he hit me, she would flog me. So, I punched Bobby the next time he tried that stunt. I guess my dear mother taught me to fight.

# Luther Samuel Stewart

## June 7, 1894 – March 21, 1979

Late in his life, I remember Dad weeping as he prayed, "Lord, I am just a common man." The phrase has stuck with me, for at that time he no doubt saw himself as just a common man. But as I think back about his life, I can only describe him as an uncommon, common man. A brief outline of the life of this uncommon man follows.

My father Luther Samuel Stewart was born on June 7, 1894, to Noah and Rachel Virginia Barber Stewart in south Cobb County, Georgia. Dad's mother died when he was only 18 months old. He was raised by his grandmother, stepmother, and father and had two older sisters and three younger half sisters. He lived on a farm in Cobb County, lived in Atlanta, and lived at Ball Ground, GA.

Luther enlisted in the army on July 17, 1917 at St. Louis, Missouri under the name of Jackson Stone. He used that name until our family moved from Iowa to Georgia in 1934.

Jackson Stone served in Company C, 36th Infantry, 12$^{th}$ Division (Plymouth Division). He was discharged on June 23, 1919 at Camp Taylor, Kentucky. His World War I Army serial number was ASN 952-809. This was copied from the family Bible.

Following is my account of my father's life as written in my journal on March 26, 1979, shortly after his death. (Volume III, page 207 ff)

An Uncommon, Common Man

Luther Samuel Stewart:
Born June 7, 1894 – Cobb County, GA
Died March 21, 1979 – Richmond County, GA

It has been a time of grief and gratitude for us these past few days. Thanksgiving and celebration were not to be excluded from a final worship service as we paid our last public tribute to Dad.

It was cold and raining hard at 10:00 AM this past Friday, March 23$^{rd}$ at Elizabeth United Methodist Church. He and Grace had attended that little church for about 30 years and they have lived in that community for more than 40 years.

It was comforting to see so many people there who came out on a cold, wet first day of spring. Among them were Harold Chastain, Chester and Ann Rogers and Mr. C. H. King, former principal of Elizabeth School. Mr. King is 90 years old but still drives a car and drove himself to the church service. I had not seen these people in at least 25 to 30 years.

I am sure that everyone at the worship service could have paid some kind of special tribute to Dad in their own special way.

The long physical and mental decline that took place in his life over the last five years slips quickly into memory's back room. But, knowing that his kidneys had ceased to function, that his heart had stopped once, that he'd had exploratory surgery and was alive only because he was plugged-in to so many machines, we could not wish him to continue "living" under these conditions.

He had obtained a seventh grade education which was probably as much, or more, than most southern children received who were born before 1900.

His strengths were honesty, the ability to listen respectfully, and to relate to all sorts and conditions of people. He loved children and as long as he lived, he enjoyed being around children. Grace said that was one of the things that had attracted her to him. Grace said he was not like the other men she knew.

Of course, he also had a temper. He could yell and carry on like a spoiled child in an adult body, if he became upset or irritated. Such is the condition of most men and thus he was a common man.

He was uncommon in that he was a person in many ways of deep and uncommon faith. He truly believed that hardship and stumbling blocks can be great teachers, if we but take the time and have the patience to learn from them.

He was uncommon in that he was regular and devout in private and corporate prayer. He and Grace read the Bible from Genesis to Revelation and they took time to pray.

He was uncommon in that as a Southerner born before 1900 he displayed, to my knowledge, absolutely no prejudice toward black folks. He did not say ugly things about blacks. He was fair and square with his black customers, as with white folks.

He was uncommon in that for 20 or more years, he neither saw nor wrote to any member of his family. Electing instead to change his name and raise a family under a different name. He worked, married, settled down, and raised a family in the Midwest following World War I rather than return to his family and friends in his native Georgia.

He was uncommon in that he had a Damascus Road conversion, became a changed man, a "born again" person, if there ever was one, and returned to his native Georgia, found his sisters, assumed his real name again and then brought his wife and four children back with him to a warmer climate. He was truly the prodigal son returned from the land of the dead.

I could never forget how these and other of Dad's experiences molded and focused my own life as an eleven or twelve-year-old boy.

He loved watching baseball games in the old Ponce de Leon ball park and in the new stadium. He enjoyed listening to the World Series on the radio and still later watching baseball on television.

We could play catch and pitch horseshoes around the gas station, for that sport could be started and stopped at any point and then picked up again.

Dad served on the local school board, served as a church officer, served as a registrar at the election polls, and did extra duty as a school bus driver during World War II.

He did not believe in credit and to the best of my knowledge he never bought anything on credit, but paid with cash.

He did not believe in insurance and never took out any kind of insurance policies. Of course, he did take out car insurance as the law required.

He did not believe in Masonic orders and he did not trust "smooth, fast-talking salesmen." And he was forced to suffer the onslaughts of plenty of the latter of these while running the store.

I remember a few stories my Dad told me about his early years. He attended Formwalt Street School in Atlanta. While living on a farm near Smyrna, he rode with his father Noah delivering milk to customers between the farm and Marietta. He said folks would come out with pitchers, pails, or jars, and the raw milk would then be poured into the customers' containers. Leftover milk would be brought back to the farm and fed to the hogs.

On another occasion, Dad told of going from Ball Ground to Nelson, GA, by himself to take part in some sort of field day activity. Dad said he won a foot race and received first prize of 50 cents. He said he ran all the way back home to Ball Ground to tell the family of his good news, only to discover that the rest of the family had gone off for the day.

Dad told of driving a team of horses or mules for a rent collector in Atlanta. He said a severe rain storm came up and then it started to hail. The hail stones frightened horses all over Atlanta and they proceeded to tear up buggies and harnesses and many ran away.

On a postcard dated January 19$^{th}$, 1913, with a Chattanooga, Tennessee, postmark to his sister Ruby Stewart, Dad states, "I guess we will go to Lookout Mountain today. Luther." This letter may have been one of the last he wrote before he changed his name to Jackson Stone. He was 19 years old at the time and running from the law and away from his family. The letter was addressed to 168 Trinity Avenue, Atlanta. Sixty years later I worked in the Trinity-Washington Building only a few feet from Aunt Ruby's 1913 address.

In August 1983 the family gathered at Jekyll Island to celebrate Grace's 80$^{th}$ birthday. Siblings all have different memories of growing up in Iowa and Georgia. My sister Pauline, who was born after we moved to Georgia, commented that life got better for the family after we moved to the new store at 1710 Church Street Extension, Marietta. Dallas commented that he was always aware of the fact that our family was just a bit better off than were his playmates at school.

Then Grace commented on how Dad did not want us to be involved in a lot of activities because that would make it appear as though we thought we were better than other people. Grace went on to say that she was determined to have us involved in as many things as possible, such as 4-H and Scouts.

Pauline practically grew up in the new store and has more memories about it than any of the rest of her siblings. She commented on Dad's smoking cigarettes and selling beer and wine, and that so far as she knew, he never went to Greer's Chapel. He also had a bad, mean temper. Grace defended him saying, "He couldn't help it." Pauline, no doubt, remembers when Dad kept the store open on Sundays.

However, later in life, Dad and my mother Grace joined the Elizabeth Methodist Church where Dad was both an active and regular member. After they closed the store in the early 1960s, the two of them would clean the church building.

Also, for a time at Battlefield Camp, he kept the store open 24 hours a day, but that did not last long. They also sold hamburgers and Grace frequently cooked breakfast for anyone who wanted it.

A few years ago, Barbara told me the children of Rachel Virginia (Winnie, Ruby, and Luther) did not live with the remainder of the family after leaving Ball Ground. The three older children lived with their Grandmother Barber in a big house, but Barbara did not know the location.

Grandmother Barber died in 1911 and Luther, Winnie, and Ruby inherited her estate, such as it was. The three rented an apartment. At some point, Dad squandered his portion of the inheritance. Ruby married George Williams and Winnie worked for the Atlanta Athletic Club.

A photo taken the day of Noah's marriage to Brunie, shows Dad seated on the arm of a chair and his left elbow on his father's shoulder.

Noah H. Stewart and Luther Stewart, August 22, 1896.

It was a contentious family. Grandmother Barber had moved in to take care of the three children when Rachel Virginia died. Luther was 18 months old at the time.

Luther's father was soon looking for a new wife. The second wife he picked, Brunie, was scarcely older than Luther's sister Winnie at the time. On the back of a photo taken on August 22, 1896, their wedding day, it states that Brunie Rateree was 16 at the time. Winnie was six at the time. Brunie would have been only ten years older than Winnie!

Young Luther Stewart's family, around 1903. Left to right:
Front row: Noah H. Stewart, Luna, Brunie (Noah's second wife),
Louise (in Brunie's lap), Grandmother Barber, and Clara.
Back Row: Winnie, Ruby, and Luther.
Grandmother Barber was the mother of Noah's first wife Rachel Virginia,
who was the mother of Winnie, Ruby, and Luther.

Grandmother Barber and Brunie never got along well from all reports. In later years, Brunie said Grandmother Barber turned the older children against her.

At any rate, Barbara told me that our Dad once said, "I want all my kids under one roof at night." And he also said, "I never had any family until I went in the army."

Barbara also reported that Dad was once stabbed with a knife. It seems he (a small fellow at the time) was walking down the street in Atlanta and some older boys lassoed him with a rope. Dad took out his knife and cut the rope. The boys then took his knife and stabbed him just above the heart and he bore that scar all his life.

I note from an old loose leaf notebook the following: Bevo Building in St. Louis, Missouri. Stationed in Worcester, Massachusetts. I also recall Dad speaking of being stationed at Fort Snelling, Minnesota. I remember Dad speaking of being in an honor guard when President Woodrow Wilson returned from the Paris peace talks. Dad did not go overseas during the war.

Luther in North Georgia around 1948

# Grace Minta Pritchard Stewart

### August 20, 1903 - June 7, 2000

I have been thinking of all that I might or should write about my mother. In my memories plus my family history files, I have more material from and about her than any other member of my immediate family: Bibles, photos, letters, cashbook, daily diary, articles she wrote that were printed in the Iowa publication *Wallaces Farmer*, plus what I have written in my journals.

She did not have an easy life. She was born and raised on the farm of her parents, George and Minnie Pritchard. Married at age 19, she was plunged from being a young teenager to being a farmer's wife with all the responsibilities that accompanied life on an Iowa farm following World War I. Plus, she had three children in short order and then a fourth by the time she was 27 years of age. Still, she did find time to write, read to her children at night, work in the garden, can vegetables, help with cow milking, and even help Dad pick corn in the fall.

Grace and Jackson Stone in Iowa, early in their marriage

When she was young, she had an opportunity to attend school in town and live with "Uncle Guy and Aunt Mettie" Courtright while in school. They even wanted to adopt her as their own, as they had no children. I understand that Grandpa Prichard was agreeable but Grandmother would have none of it.

Grace attended Iowa State Teacher's College at Cedar Falls, IA, and her picture appears in the Old Gold yearbook of 1920 in the sub-collegiate section. I doubt that she attended more than one year. I am uncertain as to whether or not she received financial aid from Uncle Guy and Aunt Mettie.

Young Grace Pritchard's family. Front row, left to right: Minnie, Blinn (in Minnie's lap), Bill, Grace, George Pritchard.
Back row: Zelda and Eddie. Martha had not been born yet.

Grace had enough training to begin teaching school and for a time taught school with a student body of exactly seven boys. I suppose it was considered more important for boys to go to school than girls, at that time.

The big gap in my knowledge of my mother is her early childhood and teen years. Part of it was spent during the war years of 1914 to 1918. She had an older sister and older brothers, so she probably was not burdened with farm work as much as her older siblings. I am indebted to my cousin Alan

Oppedal for his work in researching and writing the history of the Prichard and Capener families in his book *The Inevitable Triumph*.

One story that I remember of her early childhood that she told us many times, was an accident that happened that could have cost her life. She climbed into the manure spreader, and unseen by her father, had an easy ride. Except that she got caught in the spinning gear in the rear of the spreader and could have been killed. She claims that it did result in partial loss of vision in one eye.

Another story that Grace told about her early childhood was Aunt Becky Prothero coming to live with them. From Grace's account, it seems Aunt Becky was quite senile when she came to live with the Pritchard family. The new visitor was allowed to have the downstairs bedroom that had been the bedroom of George and Minnie. The parents moved upstairs into the bedroom of the girls and hung a sheet between the beds. There was not a lot of privacy for anyone except Aunt Becky. Grace said Aunt Becky hated the South, as she had lost a lover in the Civil War. Her brother Uncle Morton Prothero, also a civil war veteran, would come up on occasion from the Iowa Old Soldiers Home and spend time on the farm. Grace remembered him as a pipe smoker who used a magnifying glass to light his pipe. I wonder how he lit it when it was dark or the sun was not shining?

Grace said Aunt Becky would turn her back on her when she walked into the bedroom. Thus, she assumed that the visitor did not like her. Aunt Becky, Rebecca Prothero, is buried in the Ruthven Crown Hill cemetery.

I note a comment in a letter from Mary Capener Johnson in reference to their childhood days, "... Remember when we were kids having wet fall weather and the old thrashing machine would be in the yard for days..." I am sure my mother and her siblings were as excited about this big labor saving machinery as we were in the following generation and subsequent generations.

From Al Oppedal's account in *The Inevitable Triumph*, Pauline Prichard came to live with George and Minnie around 1909, when Pauline was twelve and Grace would have been six. Pauline was the daughter of John Prichard, George's father. Pauline was a half sister to George, but I am sure Grace always looked on Pauline as an older sister. Pauline had learned music while living in Kansas and was always an accomplished musician. I am sure Grace obtained some of her interest in the piano and music from Pauline. I am sure my youngest sister is named after Pauline Prichard Sampson.

## Grace Minta Pritchard Stewart

After Grace's death, my niece Rachel Tilley Fagans, Barbara's daughter wrote about her memories of Grace:

> "I have always felt close to Grandmother. She talked to me as though I were her equal from the earliest of my memories, as she talked to everyone with whom she came into contact. As equals. No matter the age, color, denomination, or sex.
>
> Quent and I lived with Grandmother and Granddaddy Stewart in the last months before we left for Venezuela. It was a special time in our lives. I remember coming in the living room and finding Grandmother and Granddaddy sitting on the couch and holding hands."

Grace Stewart, 1988

I will have more to say about Mother in the next chapters.

# The Great Transition

## 1934

From Iowa corn fields to Georgia cotton fields; frozen North to sunny South. In the transition from Yankee land to Rebel land, the Jack Stone family becomes the Luther Stewart family.

Dust bowl, the Great Depression. Dad has a Saint Paul Damascus Road conversion. In 1934 he decided to go back to Georgia to find his sister Ruby and other relatives. He found lots and lots of relatives and several came back to Iowa with him.

Shortly after his return from Georgia, Dad announced that we would be moving to Georgia. Once the crops were harvested there would be a sale of all of our farm animals, farm machinery and equipment, and most of our household goods.

Our names were to change during the trip to Georgia. We would no longer be the Stone family; our new last name would be Stewart. Dad's name would change from Jack Stone back to his birth name, Luther Samuel Stewart. I would no longer be called Francis Stone. When we arrived in Georgia at the age of 12, I would be Francis Stewart. The children's birth certificates were all changed to show the new last name of Stewart.

The sale was held on November 14, 1934. At that time we had 25 Holstein milk cows, six horses, pigs, 150 buff Leghorn chickens, and 50 pure bred Minorca chickens. A free lunch was served, but folks were to bring their own cups for coffee. As we children were in school, we did not get to see the sale take place.

By early December, Dad had acquired a 4-wheel trailer. Actually it was a regular double-box farm wagon that had been converted into a trailer. A garage mechanic in Ruthven by the name of Art Simonson had removed the wagon wheels and replaced them with automobile wheels and tires. Also, he had installed what Dad called a "fifth wheel". It simply made the trailer turn much easier.

# PUBLIC SALE

As I am moving to Georgia, I will hold a complete closing out sale on what is known as the Courtright farm, 6¼ miles north of Ruthven; 2 miles east and ¾ of a mile south of Lake Center school; 6¾ miles south and 2 miles east of Terrill, on

# Wednesday, Nov. 14
## 1934
Free Lunch at 11:30. Sale starts at 12. Bring cup for coffee.

## 41 Head of Livestock 41

### 6 Head of Horses

Sorrel gelding, 14 yrs. Gray mare, 10 yrs. Bay mare, 11 yrs. Roan Gelding, 10 yrs. One good work mare. Roan mare colt.

### 25 Head of Holstein Cattle

12 Holstein milk cows, some of these are milking heavy now, others fresh soon. 7 head of heifers, six coming 2 yrs., one ten months old. Holstein bull. 3 bull calves. 2-year old steer. Sucking bull calf.

### 10 Head of open Gilts, spotted, extra prolific

About 200 Chickens: consisting of 150 Buff Leghorns & 50 pure bred Minorcas.

### Farm Machinery, Etc.

8 ft. McCormick-Deering Binder. John Deere Mower. Deere drag. Deere 9 ft. disc. Deere planter. Deere sulky plow. 2 row Bailor Cultivator. Emerson gang plow. 2 wagons with triple boxes. Hay rack and gear. 12 x 12 ft. brooder house. 6 x 18 ft. hog house. Cream Separator. Hand corn Sheller. Cooling tank. 1½ horse h. p. gas engine and pump jack. Single row Bailor cultivator. 2 sets of harness. Collars. Several mash hoppers. Some alfalfa and wild hay in barn.

### Household Goods

Winchester circulator heater. Sanico Junior range. Dinning table and chairs. Beds. Linoleum rugs. Sewing machine. Piano. Wicker set. Wash boiler. Tub. Enameled top kitchen table. Fruit jars and all other household goods. Potatoes and other vegetables.

**and many articles too numerous to mention.**

TERMS: All sums of $10 and under cash; on sums over $10, six months time will be given on approved notes. No property to be removed until settled for, and settlement must be made on day of sale. Parties desiring credit, see clerk before day of sale.

Flyer for sale of Jackson Stone farm livestock, equipment, and other items

The trailer was loaded with Mother's Maytag washing machine, her cedar chest, lots of clothes, and lots of canned food, as she had not the foggiest idea of what was in store for us in Georgia.

We spent our last night with the Lester Sampsons, our closest neighbors. Also, we left by way of Spencer and stopped briefly with the Kinneys. I guess we had prayers for a safe journey and we were off, except we left in a snow storm. With the load being pulled by the 1929 Chevrolet, we probably made no more than 30-35 miles an hour. But we were on our way to Georgia.

We were taking a round-a-bout way to get to Georgia, as we first had to visit relatives in Texas. Nights were spent in homes open for tourists along the way. I remember nights spent in Topeka, Kansas, and Tulsa, Oklahoma.

We arrived in Texas in early December. The weather was mild and folks were bringing cotton to Ross Legg's gin in McGregor, Texas. This was my first opportunity to see cotton and to see a gin in operation. There were lots and lots of kin folks in Texas, and now we were having to learn Southern language and customs.

After spending a few days in Texas, we at last turned east toward Georgia and our new home. But before we left Texas, we were able to buy gas for eight and nine cents a gallon. Gas was cheap, partly because of the Great Depression and partly because gas had recently been discovered in East Texas and there was little market for it.

We had one more night on the road. We may have slept in the car (four kids and two adults – not much sleeping), or we may have spent the night in another tourist home near Meridian, Mississippi. As the next night approached, we were in East Alabama where oak trees lined both sides of the road for miles. This was the area now known as Valley, Alabama and where almost exactly 13 years later I would return to marry my dear wife Clarice in the Langdale, Alabama Baptist Church. But that is another story.

At age eleven I was thinking about Georgia, the place where we would be forbidden to sing "Marching Through Georgia," a Union Army song. We were traveling like Okies in Steinbeck's *Grapes of Wrath*.

Finally, late at night we managed to get through Atlanta and arrived in Fair Oaks, south of Marietta at the home of Zack and Willie Daniel. More of Dad's kin folks that we had never met or heard of before. We spent the night with Zack and Willie, wonderful folks. The next day we moved into a new house that Zack had built very recently. It was about a fourth mile from Zack and Willie and next door to Zack's brother Newt Daniel.

The house was located on top of a hill with a big open lot. A good place to have a milk cow, and it was not long before we had one. But before we bought a cow, the lot had to be cleared up. Brush was piled up and burned. Unfortunately, as I was helping burn the trash, I was from time to time in the smoke. The next day I was itching from my scalp to my toes. Another discovery in the south -- Poison Oak and Poison Ivy. The oil from the vines was in the smoke and gave me the worst case of Poison Oak I ever had.

Once we were settled in, it was time to meet more of our kinfolks. One winter day we drove over to meet some of them. They lived in a simple home with an open fireplace. I had never seen an open fireplace, since in Iowa everyone used wood stoves. I shall never forget the old woman coming to greet me with open arms. She had been dipping snuff and some of it was on her cheeks. She had to hug and kiss me. That was one of my most uncomfortable and embarrassing moments. We were not into a lot of hugging and kissing kinfolks when we lived in Iowa, and this was another adjustment to make.

After we got to Georgia, we were forbidden to sing "Marching Through Georgia." In Iowa we children used to sing that on cold winter days in school as we marched around the stove to warm up. "Tramp, tramp, tramp, the boys are marching through Georgia." But never at home with Dad around.

We bought a cow and it was my job to feed and milk her. We needed the milk with four children and baby sister Pauline arrived very soon after we got to Georgia. The lot was not fenced so I had to put her on a rope and stake her out. This required moving the stake at regular intervals. Unfortunately, the cow was not trained to the rope and frequently became entangled in it, requiring me to rescue the creature.

Now it was decided by the decision maker (namely Dad) that we (meaning Mother) could take care of an aged, sickly relative by the name of "Aunt" Sophronie Barber. We were to call her Aunt Phronie (Fronie). She was mostly bedridden and preferred to eat vanilla wafers above everything else. She died on August 6, 1935 and was buried in the Barber cemetery on the old U.S. 41 highway at Fair Oaks.

To add insult to injury, she hated Yankees. Yankees had destroyed Georgia and killed many of her kin. It was certainly no easy time for Mother. Mother was about as far from being a trained nurse as possible. She had tons of housework to do, a tiny baby, four other children to feed, and clothes to wash. Thankfully, there was no outside farm work or chores and she could handle it. She did write back to Iowa folks and said to them, "You folks don't know how lucky you are."

Thus the great transition. We had to learn lots of new words: grits, mush, hoe cake, cat-head biscuits, fatback, streak-o-lean, "come in and sit a spell," "hits down yonder," "yall come back, y' hear," "get a tow sack and tote it," "right smart", "sho nuff", and chitterlings.

To us, farming in Cobb County was almost a joke, when compared to the Iowa farming we were accustomed to. Cotton farming was done with one or two mules and a scooter plow. Fields were on slopes that required terraces to keep the land from washing down the hill and into the creeks and streams during the rainy season. Corn was not "picked" but "gathered" and fodder was pulled (leaves pulled off the corn stalks) and saved for feed in the winter.

Cotton farming and cotton picking in the 1930s were even more labor intensive than growing corn. Picking cotton by hand was a back-breaking, labor-intensive task. No wonder the South needed so many slaves to grow and harvest cotton. I have picked corn with my Dad and I have picked cotton for a penny a pound. I prefer picking corn. I never made as much as $1 a day picking cotton. It was a back-breaking job, and I never quite learned to crawl on my knees, pick the cotton, stuff it in the tow sack and move fast.

At Fair Oaks we learned to ride bicycles and rode the street cars to Marietta for five cents.

The Olive Springs School at Fair Oaks was much larger than those we had attended in Iowa. I entered the school in January 1935, one month before my twelfth birthday. I was eleven years old and in the seventh grade. The teacher talked funny and, no doubt, I looked and talked funny to her. In addition, I was taking subjects I had not taken in Iowa. Dorothy and Barbara were in grades behind me but seemed to make it fine. Dorothy was ten and in the sixth grade. Mother believed in moving us along fast!

At any rate, I was held back a grade – a great blow to my pride. I was a failure and not as smart as I thought I was. But I was reminded that I had started first grade at age five. I still have my seventh grade photo from Olive Springs. We students were a ragtag-looking bunch. The girls were in the front row and most were taller than us boys. There were ten girls, twelve boys, and our stern looking teacher.

It was about this time that Franklin D. Roosevelt made a trip to Atlanta. We were put on school busses and transported to Piedmont Park. Hundreds of students from Atlanta and nearby schools were lined up on both sides of the park road. We had a brief glimpse of FDR as he passed by in his open-topped car. It is said that when he saw the pinched faces of the students and our best, but rag-tag clothes, it inspired him to pressure the congress to pass some of his "New Deal" legislation – WPA, NRA, CCC, REA, and others. Some of this legislation was later declared unconstitutional by the Supreme Court. But FDR was always popular at our house, and we never missed one of his famous fireside chats.

Dad teamed up with another cousin, Charlie Fleming, also a World War I veteran and a veteran who drew a pension as a result of injuries on the battlefields of Europe. Charlie was a great talker. They first teamed up to sell a device called a Vicks gas saver. It was supposed to allow a car to gain far more miles to the gallon. The only hitch was Dad had to put up a bundle of money to get in on this great invention. Money from the sale of the farm, money that we could not afford to lose, but we did.

Next, Dad took a turn at selling Fuller brushes. That was a little better. At least we had lots of new brushes to bathe with and clean house.

## Battlefield Camp

Battlefield Camp was next, located on the old U.S. 41 Dixie Highway about one mile north of Big Kennesaw Mountain, the site of major Civil War battles. There we had electricity for the first time. It was a Delco system with lots of batteries. Usually, the engine to run the generator was started about dark and ran until bedtime or store closing time. Things got better at Battlefield Camp. We had a store, a house, a shed for the cow, a garage, and three or four tourist cabins to rent. There was no inside plumbing. We had ready access to groceries from the store and fresh milk.

Since we had a cow at Fair Oaks, it was my job to take the cow to Battlefield Camp. I simply walked the cow around the back roads, through Marietta and out old Kennesaw Avenue and north on old U.S. 41 to Battlefield Camp.

Some folks bought groceries on credit and paid on the weekend. Railroad section hands, hosiery mill, marble mill, and other workers. The gas pumps had ten-gallon glass tanks on top. Gas was hand pumped into the glass tanks and by gravity flowed into the car tanks. The pumps were very dangerous because a car hitting one of the glass tanks could cause a terrible fire. Also, it was difficult to gauge the exact number of gallons by looking up at the glass tank.

Still, pumping gas, putting water in a radiator, air in tires, changing tires, washing windshields, checking oil, and so forth, was a whole lot easier than milking cows on a bitterly cold winter night and shoveling manure the next day!

Barbara and Francis at the Battlefield Camp store

Dad always kept a loaded Model 97 Winchester shotgun hanging on the wall above the bed where he and Mom slept. One night a passing heavy truck shook the ground and the store, and the shotgun went off over their heads. Dad woke up and shouted, "Someone's shooting at us! Hand me the gun." The gun had fallen to the floor. When Dad reached for the shotgun and it was not there he yelled, "They've stolen the gun!"

The Battlefield Camp store is no longer there. It was next to the Brushy Mountain battlefield, which is on maps. I collected lots of minnie balls and some cannon balls at the Brushy Mountain battlefield site.

## Olive Springs School

Olive Springs School was quite different from Lake Center School in Iowa. It was located just south of Marietta on the streetcar line from Marietta to Atlanta. Today, it would be called a suburban community. However, I was not thinking in those terms in 1935.

Mr. Robert L. Osberne was principal. Every morning he led the school in a brief worship service, usually repeating the Lord's Prayer and perhaps some brief passage of scripture.

Some of the students called him 'fessor' Osberne. He had a little hand bell that he used to start school and to call students in from the playground after recess. Some of the mischievous boys would attempt to divert his attention, unscrew the handle of the bell, and remove the clapper. I suppose they hoped to get a longer recess that way.

One other thing, Mr. Osberne was a bachelor and had a room with our neighbor who had a famous name, John Wilkes Booth. On occasion, we would see him at the Booth residence. He owned a microscope. It was the first one I had ever seen. Not only did he show it to us, but he let us view a redbug (chigger) under it. It was an ugly red thing with sharp claws, as I recall.

I don't remember much about the seventh grade, except for the teacher Miss Ruby Sewell, and the fact that she flunked me. It was a very embarrassing experience, especially, since both of my sisters made it through their grades after moving from Iowa. Anyway, I was to spend two years in the seventh grade. We soon moved to Battlefield Camp and I was away from Olive Springs.

One other educational experience from the Booth family was their son's large collection of boys' books that were left with his parents when he moved out. His sister loaned me the books. There were lots and lots of Tom Swift books, as I recall.

Our closest neighbors, the Sarboroughs, helped us identify some of the flowers, trees and shrubs that we had never seen until moving to Georgia: dogwoods, jonquils, pine trees, broom sedge, honeysuckle, and others. This was just before kudzu was introduced from Japan and took over in the South, so I learned about that all-encompassing vine later.

I am sure we walked to school as we were no more than a half mile from the school, but I do not recall any experiences with the daily round-trip. Playground activities consisted mainly of baseball.

This school was later named Robert L. Osberne School and probably was later torn down and replaced with another Robert L. Osberne school. I do remember a Mr. "C" the janitor who always swept the hallways at the end of the day. He put down some kind of compound that made sweeping easier. It was an oily compound that impregnated the wood. I believe it was later outlawed, as it would make the wood burn very fast and hot if the floors caught fire. However, with so many kids coming in the room from home and walking along red clay streets, I am sure lots of mud and dirt were tracked in every single day. The Japanese are smarter. Kids have to take off their shoes before entering the school room.

# The Store

We moved from Battlefield Camp in 1938 to the new store, a service station and grocery store, approximately one and a half miles south toward Marietta on U.S. 41 and located at 1710 Church Street Extension. The new store was known as Stewart Service Station.

I do not remember the move. We no longer kept a cow. If I had led a cow up U.S. 41, I no doubt would have remembered it. Anyway, the new store had no barn in which to keep a cow.

This was our first home with indoor plumbing. From 1922 when Dad and Mother were married until 1938 they had never lived in a home with indoor toilets or running water. Moreover, the store had electricity (no Delco battery system) and it was used.

Neon lights on the east and west side over the covered car port said "Woco Pep" in red. In addition, a big round neon sign on the south side below the gable said "Pure". This was in blue.

For a family of seven it was still small for living space. There was a tiny kitchen and dining room on the first floor and just off the store. Stair steps from the kitchen led down to two bedrooms. The east bedroom was Mother and Dad's and the west one was for the girls. That left no bedroom for Dallas and me, but it was quickly solved by building a small eight-by-ten foot room on the back porch. It was not big enough for a double bed and dresser so a bunk bed and dresser were installed.

There was no laundry room, but that was solved by sending laundry out to Nellie McConnell, a fine black lady. She would send her nephew Raymond over with a laundry basket and written instructions for any groceries she wanted. Her writing was much worse than mine and sometimes it would take every member of the family to figure out what she wanted.

As for my penmanship, it has never been so hot. Some years ago, while talking with old classmates at Kennesaw, they said the teacher asked me to read what I had written on the blackboard, but I could not read it either. I suppose that is why my parents were willing to swap the old Model 97 Winchester shotgun that had been used to hunt pheasants in Iowa for a typewriter. This was so I could take a high school business class that included typing and shorthand.

The store itself had a good supply of groceries. The north wall had shelves that went up eight or ten feet. Since the store had 12-foot ceilings there was plenty of shelf room. On the shelves were canned goods and flour, both plain and self-rising in cotton bags. Cornmeal, always white and never yellow, came from local millers. One miller was Chester Rogers' father.

Shelves were also on both sides of the west window. These shelves had a variety of tobaccos: chewing, dipping, and smoking (Bull Durham, Dukes Mixture), plug tobacco (Brown's Mule, Day's Work, and others), and Brewton snuff. Other shelves held such items as Epsom salt, aspirin tablets, mineral oil, turpentine, iodine, Band-aids, and so forth.

The cash register was on the counter near the west window. To the right of the cash register and toward the north wall was a nice glass showcase with candy, candy bars, and chewing gum.

In front of these shelves and to the side of the cash register nearest the south wall was a simple icebox with a lid. Fifty-pound blocks of ice were delivered nearly every day in summer months to keep the Coca Colas, Dr. Peppers, 7-Ups, Orange Crush, and Pepsi Colas cold. Only later did Dad acquire an electric refrigerator box.

Under the big south window was a small shelf for displays and under-shelf space was enclosed and used for storing quart cans of motor oil. However most oil was sold in bulk from a storage tank outdoors that was enclosed in a shed.

To the right as a person entered the store was a refrigerator, in which meat was kept: cube steak, pork chops and other meats. Salted meat, fatback, and streak-o-lean were kept in an open wooden box.

Another counter with scales ran east-west in front of the north wall. As I recall, hoop cheese was kept on this counter. At a later date, well after 1938, the cash register was kept on this counter.

Prices for food around 1938 and 1940 I well remember: Double Q salmon, two cans for 25 cents; bread 10 cents a loaf, soft drinks 5 cents, candy bars 5 cents; sardines, small can 5 cents and a large can 10 cents; Vienna sausage 5 cents; small box of crackers 5 cents and a large one-pound box 10 cents. For 15 cents a person could buy a Hershey bar, a box of crackers (or a pack of peanuts), and a Coca Cola. I could pay for that by picking 15 pounds of cotton.

The three outside gasoline pumps were electric and we no longer had the 10-gallon glass tanks that had to be filled by hand pumping. The three grades of gas were economy, regular, and ethyl. Ethyl was the most expensive and contained lead.

Kerosene was kept outside in a tank with a hand pump. A lock was put on it at night. Also outside, was an oil room for grease and bulk oil. This was near the grease rack, which was used for changing oil and lubricating cars. I did my share of changing oil, lubricating cars, changing and inflating tires, replacing fan belts and radiator hoses.

We also carried inner tubes, some tires, and boots. We did not carry very many tires, as we had no place to store them. Plus, it would have been stock that did not turn over rapidly. An air compressor was kept next to the kerosene tank on the west side of the store.

Changing a tire required the use of one or more tire irons and a rubber hammer to remove the tire from the rim and again to replace the tire on the rim. Occasionally it would take a lot of beating and banging to remove and replace the tire. I still have, as of 1999, Dad's old rubber hammer with its homemade handle. I wonder how many times it was used to change tires. Now a tire shop can remove, replace and balance a tire in a very few minutes.

At first Dad tried to keep the store open 24 hours a day, but that required some hired help. Even a family of seven could not do it. There was little traffic on old U.S. 41 after midnight and the 24-hour effort was not continued. However, Dad did keep the store open on Sundays for many years, and I suppose he began to close on Sundays during the World War II gas rationing years, but I was not living at home then.

Likewise, he felt it necessary to sell beer and wine to promote his business. I am sure as minors Dorothy and I sold our share of it, but that was before the law prohibited it, at least that is what I think.

## Sales Vendors

Bread, oil, gasoline, notions, meats and soft drinks were delivered regularly by vendors, including the "bread man," "Toms Peanut man," Lance crackers. Mr. Pause brought meats, cheese, bologna, hot dogs, fatback, and streak-o-lean meat. He bought his meats from a firm in Atlanta called Tennenbaum. Mr. Pause carried his meats in the back of his car with the back seat removed. He also carried a supply of other things, such as Epsom salt. He had the route for many years and he and Dad became close friends.

Claude Jordan delivered gasoline. Taft Owenby took orders for the wholesale company, Veach Groceries. Grady Veach had bought the wholesale firm from Dad's cousin Zack Daniel. Taft Owenby later became a Baptist preacher and was pastor of the Sandy Plains Baptist Church for many years. The old wholesale grocery store located next to the railroad tracks, across the street from the train station is now used as an antique shop. I am sure this is one of the oldest buildings near the Marietta square.

At other times, Dad would drive his pickup truck into Marietta and pick up his supplies directly from the Veach wholesale grocery store. Dad did not take to new salespeople at first. They all had to prove themselves in some way before he bought from them. In other words, he had to learn to trust the people who sold him goods before they got any money from him.

## The Regulars

The regular customers were the folks who kept Dad in business and food on the table for the rest of us. They too, at times became somewhat of an extended family, or simply a vital part of our lives. Paris Hill was a truck driver for a company called Frank North. The materials Paris hauled had a strong odor and much of it clung to Paris. But, Paris was an honest man. One of the few black truck drivers I knew back before 1940 was Guy Asbury, a one-armed black man who traded regularly with us and who lived only about a half mile from the store.

Chester Rogers delivered the old Atlanta Georgian and later worked for the Marietta Journal. Chester and his wife became very close friends and they were folks Mother always wanted to visit in later years when she came back from Florida on a visit. The Rogers later bought the Battlefield Camp store, where they lived for a number of years.

There was a railroad section gang. A black section crew lived in section houses next to the railroad tracks, located next to the U.S. 41 overpass about one mile north of the station. I don't remember their names, but they were regular customers. One had the nickname of Geech. Sometimes folks would torment him by slipping up behind him and tickling him. Geech would jump and flail his arms about. You would have to be careful or you would get a sharp blow for such an unkind act.

Jim Brock's wife often came over to help Mother. I believe his sons became fairly successful business men in Marietta. Barbara said he later became the first black man to serve on a jury in Cobb County.

Freeman Brooks and his wife Sally moved up north to work during World War II, and I doubt if they ever came back to Georgia.

Jack and Dan Myers were fine friends. Jack became chief of the fire department in the town of Kennesaw. I believe both dropped out of school before high school. Sometimes we would sit on the bank on Sunday afternoon to watch cars go by and occasionally we would spy a woman with her skirt pulled up well above her knees. That was excitement for us in those days.

Willie Gilbert and his parents lived just west of the mountain. Their farm property today is now part of a subdivision and some of the most valuable property in the county. They were fine folks who never had a lot of money but had the reputation of being as honest as the day is long.

Mr. and Mrs. Whitlock and their sons Harold and Cecil were regulars. Harold later established an accounting firm that is still in business on old Kennesaw Road. Cecil moved to Pickens County and built a large house to accommodate his parents or in-laws. He later sold the home and land to the Huber Corporation for a large sum of money. The Huber Corporation used the home for their headquarters while they opened a new marble quarry near Marble Hill.

Mack Greenway was our school bus driver. He had an old Model A Ford truck with a wooden bus body. Mack had four routes for Kennesaw school. Since we lived near him, we rode the first bus in the morning and the fourth at night, making a long day at school for us. Later we walked or rode bikes and beat the bus home in the evening.

In wintertime, some of the dirt roads were very slippery. I remember getting out to push the bus. The place where we got stuck was located on what is now the four-lane Barrett Parkway, near an automobile sales lot.

Mack's old Model A Ford bus leaked a lot of oil. In fact, we joked that it used as much oil as gas, usually two to three quarts each day. The front wheel wobbled back and forth so that it must have been difficult to steer. When we stayed at school for the fourth bus route back home in the afternoon, we would play ball behind the Kennesaw school. We could look out across the cemetery and watch for the return of the bus in the distance. Usually the bus would be followed by a cloud of dust, if the weather was dry.

## The Store

Other regulars were the Congers: Orie, Cleber and Harold. All three liked to talk and drink beer or wine. Cleber, unfortunately drank too much wine and, no doubt, used money for wine that he should have been spending on his large family. I am sure he was one of the persons who helped persuade Dad to stop selling beer and wine. However, one of the prominent doctors used to come out from town in the afternoon to drink his share of beer.

The Kendricks, Raines, Rakestraws, and Hitts were also regulars. Mike Rakestraw had somewhat of a celebrity status as he had served a hitch in the infamous Georgia chain gang. He seemed like a nice guy to us although I do not recall that we saw much of him. Mrs. Hitt, a widow with three children, had a struggle to raise her family. Horace Watkins was another regular. Naturally, Mother and Dad knew all of these people and I'm sure there were many others.

Years later after the store was closed, I found a large number of order books stored out back in the old chicken house. Each pad had the name of the person who was purchasing groceries on credit. The pad had a carbon sheet and thus a carbon copy was made for the customer to keep each time groceries were purchased. I did not know the names of the people and I later disposed of the pads. A collection agency did manage to collect quite a bit of money for Mom and Dad after the store was closed.

Tourists were a minor factor in the business although we were located on U.S. 41, which ran from Michigan to Florida. I remember Dad taking me out of high school one spring to drive a couple to Illinois. The man had suffered a heart attack and needed someone to drive them back home. I drove them to Champaign, Illinois, and then returned home by bus. It was the week of the Kentucky Derby and I stopped over to see the race. I rode the street car out to the grounds early in the morning and got a standing position on the rail. I watched the races all day and finally the derby. It was just another horse race to me and that is the one and only horse race I ever attended.

One truck driver who came to the store was from Ty Ty, GA. He hauled fertilizer from Atlanta to Sand Mountain, Alabama, in the spring, watermelons to Kentucky later in the year, and hauled coal back from Kentucky. Thus he had a load both ways. He bought a lot of gas and I know Dad appreciated his business.

One more thought about our regular customers. On weekends and paydays we were really busy. Every available member of the family waited on customers: filling grocery orders, changing oil on the grease rack, and so forth. At these times, if a tourist stopped by for gas or snacks, one of the regular customers would pump gas, check oil, take their money, bring it in for a family member to make change, and then take the change back to the visitor. In other words the regulars felt that it was their store too!

There were a few tricksters or flimflammers, but not many. One trick that Dad had repeatedly warned us kids about was pulled off by three to four men who would come in all going to different places in the store asking a lot of questions and buying one or two items. One would pay for a 49 cent item with a $20 bill. We would then make change of $19.51 cents. A few minutes later with all the hustle and bustle and questions, the guy would say, "Here, I just found the exact change. Here is 49 cents. Give me the $20 back." At that point, we would call Dad for help. It was tried on us only one time and, as I recall, and it did not work.

Then there were colorful characters: The Goat Man who has had books written about him, and so far as I know, was living in a nursing home in Macon and was nearly 100 years old in 1999. I remember one hitchhiker who bummed several regulars one day for a "tailor made" cigarette. He was offered "roll-your-own" Bull Durham, or something else. With that the bum said, "No thanks, I will use my own," and proceeded to pull out his own Camel or Lucky Strike cigarette and smoke it. He may have been the same man who hitchhiked in both directions.

He would cross back and forth across the road, depending on where the cars were coming from and hold out his thumb. He did not care where he was going, so long as he was going someplace else. Perhaps where he would have better luck bumming his choice of cigarettes.

Fairly often, a hitchhiker would ask for food. Mother was somewhat of a soft touch, she never turned anyone away. Except there was a catch, they were given some work to do while she prepared the meal for them. They were to pull weeds, cut grass, or whatever else Grace had in the back of her mind that should be done. If they were not willing to spend 20 to 30 minutes working, they were not ready for one of her meals.

Rudy York, "The Atco Slugger," stopped by the store on several occasions. Rudy was a star baseball player for the Detroit Tigers back in the 1930s. He was a tall man who hit a lot of home runs one year.

Only two customers that I recall had chauffeur drivers. One was the owner of King Edward Cigars. I think he wanted to see if we sold his brand. Another was a black man, Eddie Anderson, who went by the name of Rochester on the old Jack Benny radio show. A black man with his own chauffeur was a real oddity in those days.

My youngest brother David was born in 1942. He was a very welcome member of the family, as by that time we older children were beginning to move out on our own.

Grace and Luther Stewart in Marietta around 1970

In 1962, Dad and Mother closed the store. Dad kept tax records and the records for 1956 show he paid $167.71 Federal income tax, as noted from his cancelled check dated March 14, 1957. In 1956, he reported a net profit of $2,790.43 and total sales for the year of $25,930.49. The net profit included $390 income from rental property. Taxes paid on property amounted to $129.90. In 1957 Dad reported a business profit of $2,708.91 and other income of $480 from rental on two properties, one for $180 and the other for $300.

In 1961 Dad paid the IRS $271.65 and in 1962 he paid $240.80. Since he closed the store early in the year, he evidently managed to collect quite a lot through the bill collection company he had contracted with.

In today's dollars, their net 1956 income seems quite small, but it should be remembered that gas was around 25 or 30 cents a gallon and groceries were about what they were back in the late 1930s. In 1956, with a family of four children, my income was $3,600 a year plus what Clarice earned at the hospital and as a private duty nurse. Stamps were either three or four cents for a first-class stamp.

## The CCC Boys

The Civilian Conservation Corps (CCC) camp was located less than a half mile from the store on Old Kennesaw Avenue, which was the main road to Marietta during the Civil War. They worked on Kennesaw Mountain and over to Cheatam Hill, locating and rebuilding the battle breastworks used by both the Union and Southern armies. It was manual labor with picks and shovels – no trenching equipment in those days.

They earned about one dollar a day and were expected to send most of that home each month. They had little money to spend for candy, cigarettes, and soft drinks.

However, they did manage to discover quite a few bullets, shell casings, buttons, and other metal and lead objects that were strewn around the 1864 Civil War battlefield. Dad let the CCC boys barter for candy, soft drinks, and snacks at the store and quite a number of Civil War relics found their way to Dad's store.

I do not know how many CCC boys were stationed at Kennesaw Mountain, probably no more than 40 to 50, but they were mostly farm boys and not the least bit afraid of manual labor, for they were used to it.

As the war clouds gathered later, I am sure that many of them enlisted to serve their country that had been of so much help to them and their families during the Great Depression.

## Kennesaw School

We attended Kennesaw School for several years while living both at Battlefield Camp and the new Stewart Service Station on old U.S. 41 Highway. Kennesaw was a red brick two-story building. The auditorium was upstairs with classrooms on the first floor. The principals were Sam Mashborn and Marvin Buice.

Mashborn walked with a limp but he insisted on discipline. Once he caught Guy Willbanks and Ervin Kirkendall jumping out the window. He told them to crawl back in the window and then gave them both a whipping. However, they were very large boys and I doubt if the whipping did any damage or had much effect. Corporal punishment in schools was an accepted and common form of punishment at that time.

Marvin Buice smoked a cigar. I don't remember much about him except he said he was from Forsyth County, a county that had no black folks living in it. He said that a "nigger" could come into Forsyth County to work but had to leave the county before sundown. I don't know why that stuck in my mind all these years, but it was the thinking and part of the culture of the day.

Basketball was played on an outdoor gravel court that was very hard on basketballs and playing baseball. We always played on an indoor court during tournament time.

A few years ago, a former classmate gave me a newspaper clipping of our basketball team at tournament time. I remember a tall slim referee, a Methodist preacher by the name of Charles Allen who was pastor of the Acworth Methodist Church. He later became pastor of an Atlanta Methodist church and later a pastor out in Texas. He had a thick southern drawl, but was a well known and very popular preacher in later years. He also wrote several books, but I remember him in the late 1930s only as a tournament referee.

Baseball also was played out on a gravel field by a graveyard. If I remember correctly, the outfield was next to the graveyard.

We did have plays in the auditorium. Blackface minstrels were in vogue. I remember my mother commenting, the boys did not have to make up a dialect, they simply used their every day language. There was one other play where I had to wear a dress and smoke a cigar. I don't remember why, but I was a man dressed up like a woman, and then I had to hide a cigar in my skirt pocket, pull it out and light it.

One spring day, the sky became very dark, black and ugly. In a few hours we learned of the terrible Gainesville, Georgia, tornado that destroyed much of downtown Gainesville and took many lives.

Kennesaw School burned while I was in the ninth grade. We were then bussed to Acworth, where we attended classes in an old upstairs classroom building. I never learned what caused the fire at Kennesaw School. But, I know the same kind of floor sweeping compound was used at Kennesaw that was used at Olive Springs School.

## Acworth High School

I graduated from Acworth High School in 1940. Our class has had a large number of class reunions over the years. I have many fond memories of that school. This is true, although I attended Acworth only slightly more than two years.

Perhaps the subjects I remember most and enjoyed the most were government and plane geometry. Both were taught by Superintendent W. P. Sprayberry. Behind his back some of us called him "soup lip," but he was well liked and highly respected by most of the students. Our geometry classes were upstairs in the old building.

There were only about a dozen of us in the class. We were given an assignment at the end of each day, and the next morning we were all to go to the board and write out the problem and know the solution.

Usually Mr. Sprayberry would be late for class, but we expected him to be late and went ahead with our work at the blackboards. He called on Ty Rutledge frequently and called him "Tyrus." Ty was a sort of jokester and Mr. Sprayberry would keep a tight rein on him by making him explain how he arrived at the answer to the problem.

Miss Higgins taught a course in journalism. The product of the course was our high school yearbook, a book that I still have and treasure. A Miss Skinner taught English as I recall. Miss Bassett taught shorthand, bookkeeping, and typing. I took all three of these courses and it was there I first learned to type, a skill that has been useful to me for over 60 years and is still useful as I bang away on this computer. She was young, good looking and big breasted. J. M. Pitner, at a class reunion once said to her, "I always had trouble finding the home keys on the typewriter. You would then put your arms around my back and place my hands on the proper keys. Meanwhile I would rest the back of my head on your two pillows."

Acworth was the first and only school we attended that had an indoor gym. Basketball was almost a year-round sport, although we did have track and baseball in the flat below the school. The gym was also used as a study hall and Miss Kate, a very elderly lady, kept study hall. If we got to talking too much, she would start rapping on her book with her pencil. She was a kindly lady who was greatly respected.

We had a senior class play, "Antics of Andrew," and I had a part in it as a preacher. Edward Kemp had a lead part in it. However, both Edward and I had forgotten all about the play or that we had a part in it, until Margaret

Orr Harwick brought to a reunion a copy of the play program that she had kept all these years.

We also had a senior class banquet. Some had wanted a senior class dance, but W. P. vetoed that idea. Anyway the senior class banquet was, as I recall, the only time Dad let me use the family car for a date. My date was Nellie B. McCray, who was voted the most attractive girl in the senior class.

I picked her up at her home and after the banquet, I started to drive her home only to have a flat tire. A good excuse to park on a date. However, the tire went flat only one block from downtown Acworth and a policeman was there in moments to help me change the tire. So much for parking with my date.

I was active in the 4-H club and was fortunate to receive a 4-H scholarship for college after graduation. In 4-H club I had the following projects: corn (raised on Dennis Sharp's land), a poultry project, a pig project, and a craft project. I built a desk of poplar and the wood warped.

Francis with his 4-H Club project pig.

There were 54 of us in the senior class who graduated in the spring of 1940. At our most recent class reunions, only about a dozen were in attendance. A few (a very few) have never attended a single reunion. However, a substantial number still live in and around Cobb County and the greater Atlanta area. As of 1999, all but 16 were still living. However, we have lost track of two and do not know if they are still living.

D. F. Nations was killed in WW II in the Battle of the Bulge. He was also one of the first from our class to enter the service. Most of the male members of the class who could pass the physical exam were in one of the branches of the armed services during World War II.

Six classmates and many family members attended the 70th reunion of the Acworth High School Class of 1940 on Wednesday, October 20th, 2010: Hilbert Berry, Grady Gee, Sarah McDaniel Kemp, Nellie B. McCray Taylor, Evelyn Tumlin Crittendon, and Francis Stewart.

# New York World's Fair

## 1939

The year before I finished high school, I attended the World's Fair in New York. My Aunt Ruby was staying with her sister Aunt Winnie, Uncle Edward, and their son Bobby Abbott, who lived in an apartment in Kew Gardens on Long Island, New York. If I remember correctly, I rode a bus to New York.

Aunt Ruby wanted me to see all of the sights of New York as well as the World's Fair out in Flushing Meadows. We rode the subway, attended a movie, "Captain's Courageous," with Spencer Tracy and Freddie Bartholomew in Radio City Music Hall. The most exciting part was seeing the high-kicking Rockettes. We went up in the Empire State Building for a view of the city.

Aunt Ruby took Bobbie and me out to the World's Fair for a day. She took a picture of us in front of the Trylon and Perisphere. I remember the Russian and Italian buildings, but little about what we saw around the grounds, other than we did a lot of walking and looking.

That was my big vacation, for the next summer I spent at Fair Oaks running a filling station 16 hours a day seven days a week and sleeping in the store. It was a rather isolated and lonely job, but I survived it.

In December 1995, my sister Pauline gave me a book *1939 The Lost World of the Fair*. It has helped refresh my memory about several exhibits including Borden's, Eastman Kodak, Westinghouse, and a bit more about Aunt Winnie and Uncle Edward Abbott's apartment in Kew Gardens.

The Borden's exhibit featured a state-of-the-art milking parlor. It was a far cry from what my sister Dorothy and I experienced in Iowa. The Borden's cows walked up a ramp into a stainless steel parlor where they were fed and milked with milking machines that piped the milk into a cooling tank. It was very similar to what is used today on the large commercial dairy farms.

The Westinghouse exhibit had a big gadget that simulated a lightning strike. Very impressive! The Kodak exhibit had a replica of the larger ball and trylon that was a perfect back-drop for taking pictures and it was at this spot that Ruby made a photo of Bobbie Abbott and myself.

At the time, I was impressed with the Kew Gardens apartment of the Abbotts, but when Dad and I returned to New York some 10 years later for Aunt Winnie's funeral, I was struck by how barren and sparse the apartment seemed. Perhaps the family had fallen on hard times for whatever reason I do not know. This was in the late 1940s or early 1950s while I was still at Crozer seminary. She was buried in a large cemetery, and I suspect it would be next to impossible to find her grave today.

That is about the extent of my memories of the 1939 World's Fair. Fortunately, I have Pauline's book that gives the background and history of the development of Flushing Meadows and the entire history of the two years the fair was open. I recall attendance was 120,000 on the big fair sign the day we attended. But the book says the Fair operated at a big loss. War clouds were gathering and by 1940 Hitler was in his mad pursuit of total domination of Europe.

# University of Georgia

After graduation from Acworth High School in the spring of 1940, I entered the University of Georgia at Athens in the fall. During the summer to earn money, my father had me working in the filling station at Fair Oaks, south of Marietta, on the streetcar line. As I was the only person to operate the store, I worked 16-hour days and slept in the store. I had some kind of hot plate to cook my meals. It was a long day and a lonely job as I did not know the people who stopped for gas, bread, soft drinks, and candy.

I did get to know the man who operated a refrigerator and appliance store next door, but that was about it. There was a grocery store across the road, as I recall. The store was located only about 100 yards from the cemetery where my Great-grandfather William Barber was buried, but I did not know that at the time. Zack Daniel had a wholesale grocery store behind the filling station, and no doubt, Zack owned the filling station but I did not know that and never bothered to ask who owned the building.

Anyway, my heart was set on getting out of the filling station business and after three months I was ready to go. Dad gave me some money and I had a 4-H Club scholarship to pay part of my college expenses.

I wanted to study to be a county agent, as I enjoyed 4-H Club work, projects, and the camping experiences. One of the camps was located at the foot of Tray Mountain in northeast Georgia. There was a lake at the camp and I remember winning the rock-skipping contest on the lake. I also remember climbing up Tray Mountain, a rather easy climb as I recall.

Camp Wilkins on the University of Georgia campus appealed to me. We had opportunities to walk around the campus and visit famous Sanford Stadium, built 1928 or 1929. It looked awfully big to me, but it is much larger today and will seat more than 90,000 enthusiastic football fans.

With my 4-H background and a 4-H scholarship, I applied for and received an award for room and board at the 4-H Club home on Lumpkin Street. Actually, it was a former residence. There were at least two other 4-H Club homes in Athens at the time. One was for girls and another for boys.

The Lumpkin Street 4-H Club home was up a slope and had several large trees in the big front yard where we played catch and touch football. Later this building was torn down and the whole area graded down and turned into a practice football field.

There were some 18 or 20 of us in the 4-H Club home. Some of the bunk beds were triple-deckers as I recall. The largest room had eight or ten boys in it. We had a black man as cook and housekeeper. He was a friendly man and well liked, but he had to spend a lot of time preparing meals for such a large crowd. Perhaps some of the other boys had to help with the cooking, but I don't recall that I ever did.

Some of the men in the 4-H home whose names I recall are Idus English from northeast Georgia (His father was in the Georgia General Assembly) and Fayette McElhannon who started college at Rabun Gap and later transferred to UGA.

Fayette took flying lessons as did Idus, and both served as pilots in WWII. Fayette later became a surgeon with a big practice in Athens. His girlfriend at the time was Daisy. He always said they would get married and have 12 kids. They did get married but stopped at nine children. Three of his children also became physicians.

Jack Nix was in ROTC (Reserve Officers' Training Corps) in cavalry. Jack, in later years became State School Superintendent. Raymond Cook, a slow-talking, easy-going fellow, became a vocational agriculture teacher. Poteet from Ringgold, GA, became a school principal in his home community. Buford Torrance from Baldwin County served in the Military Police in WWII and later did volunteer work with young people in Baldwin County. Reno Tyre and Billy Gerrard are two others that I recall.

Billy became a preacher and later started a spiritual retreat center in northeast Georgia near the community of Tiger. Renfroe Comer, Ellis Kitchens and Roland Roberts were from Gray, GA. James Hardy was another resident that I recall.

Although we stayed in the 4-H home, I don't recall that any of us were engaged in farming after WWII.

I had a hard time with my college class work, just barely passing, although I did study hard. English was difficult and chemistry was horrible. I never learned the periodic table and the math required was way over me. I enjoyed the lab work in old Conner Hall. One Poultry Science project was to caponize a rooster. He looked rather weak and sickly after being turned from a rooster into a capon, but our instructor assured us that he would recover.

# University of Georgia

I believe Military Science was another required course. We were issued heavy blue uniforms and a cap that we had to wear all year during drill days, which was very hot in the springtime. However, it was a great uniform to wear when I hitchhiked from Athens to Atlanta and home. We were easily recognized, and we never had to stand on the road for more than a few minutes before we had a ride.

We did a lot of walking, as some of our classes were on the main campus and some on Ag Hill (Agriculture Hill). We walked down Lumpkin Street and across to Ag Hill. We had to walk down the hill and up another hill to the main campus for English classes and chapel. Chapel was required for freshmen, as I recall. A few students had cars, but they were mostly fraternity types. None of us in the 4-H home ever had a car.

Freshmen had to undergo the indignity of being "rat courted." We were usually pulled out of bed at 1 or 2 AM when Reno Tyre came in after having a few-too-many beers to drink. Once I was so sound asleep at 2 AM that I was carried, bed and all, out to the hall before I woke up.

Another indignity was the annual "shirt tail" parade when all the freshmen on campus had to go trouserless in a parade from the main campus out to the girls campus at the edge of town. Naturally we were accompanied by a lot of loud upperclassmen to see that we made it out there, a distance of a mile or so. Fortunately, there were enough upperclassmen with cars to bring us back after the "parade."

Naturally, we did socialize with the girls in the girls' 4-H Club home. We did not have any money to entertain them, such as going to a movie, but we did socialize.

At the end of my freshman year at UGA, I was recruited into a job selling Bibles for the Southwestern Publishing Company out of Nashville, Tennessee. Roy Steadham was my partner. Roy had sold Bibles the summer before and was to get a percent of all my sales in addition to his sales. We traveled to Nashville after school was out for a few days training at Nashville. Then we were off to North Carolina, hitchhiking across the mountains by way of Knoxville and Asheville. Our destination was Henderson, NC, a farming area north and east of Durham and near the Virginia state line. We had little success in that area and Roy suggested we try the tobacco country, specifically Robeson County, the largest county in NC and with lots of tobacco farmers.

Robeson county had a lot of Indian (Native American) farmers. It was in this area where I spent most of the summer of 1941. I made only enough money for the following fall quarter, and then with no more money, I had to drop out of school. The story of selling Bibles is a chapter in itself, which comes later.

ROTC and other class work continued in the fall, I remember getting dizzy while marching and fell out. An ROTC officer by the name of Walter Ruark came to my aid. Walter was a football lineman on the first team. His nickname was Big Chief. He suggested I not try to march anymore that day. As an ROTC officer, Walter was pulled into WWII early on. He was killed in the Battle of the Bulge in Europe. Walter was from Bostwick, GA, and years later I met Walter's parents at Gibbs Memorial Baptist Church in Bostwick, where I served as pastor for a time while a student at Mercer.

One episode that I recall from my sophomore year at UGA was another rat court. Only this time I was the judge and ended up in a heap of trouble. One evening at the supper hour, it was announced that the other boys' 4-H home was calling on us for reinforcements. Twin freshmen in that home absolutely refused to be rat-courted. They were big strong boys and threatened any upperclassmen who dared order them around. So all 18 or 20 of us walked over to the other boys' 4-H home. The twins had barricaded their rooms with the dresser and chairs against the door. However, they had no curtains over the windows and we could see them inside their room.

We managed to get in and quickly overcome the twins. Then someone said, "Who wants to be the judge?" I volunteered for the job. Then the question was asked, "Who wants to be the executioner?" Ellis Kitchens volunteered for that job. A chair was placed on top of the table and I climbed up into the judge's chair, and sentenced the twins to twenty licks each.

The next day during the noon meal we were informed that we were all to report to Dean Tate's office at 4:30 PM. At the appointed hour, the entire crowd from two homes was at the dean's office. However, there so many of us that we were sent into one of the classrooms. The dean kept us waiting for half an hour, I suppose to increase our anxiety level.

When the dean came into the room he did not appear to be the least bit happy. He proceeded to lecture us about hazing, about the rules we had broken, and then began to ask some questions. No one seemed to have any answers. Finally he said, "Well you must have had a judge. Who was the judge?" I raised my hand said, "I was the judge." He then asked me, "Who told you to be the judge?" I replied, "No one, I volunteered to be the judge." He replied, "Oh, a volunteer judge." He then asked who was the executioner and Ellis Kitchens owned up to this task.

Finally, after more lecturing, the dean told us he was putting our entire 4-H home on probation for the rest of the quarter, and if he had word of any more trouble from us, we would all be expelled. With that, I breathed a sigh of relief. I had feared that I might be expelled immediately, and I dreaded to think what my Dad might say if he saw me walking into the store after being expelled from the University of Georgia.

At the end of his lecture, the dean began to talk about the old days at the University when some boys carried pistols with them to college and when others attempted to haze them they shot their pistols. The result was that several boys jumped out of second-story windows and broke their legs. He also told of boys being taken out to the nearby cemetery and being chained to tombstones for the night. In other words, the good dean let us know that he understood where we were coming from, but that our actions would not be tolerated.

Dean Tate was Dean of Men at the university for many more years. He ushered and protected Charlene Hunter and Hamilton Holmes into the university campus as they were being threatened by white students. A man of conviction and courage, he protected the first black students to enter the university. Hamilton Holmes later became a prominent surgeon in Atlanta and Charlene Hunter Gault is a well-known commentator for National Public Radio.

On another occasion at UGA, the students marched on the governor. Gene Talmadge was governor and he made a stink about a black man coming to speak at the School of Journalism. Dean Hocking had invited the man to speak. Governor Talmadge, the rabid segregationist, put pressure on the Board of Regents and had Hocking fired. This led to a bigger stink coming from the National Accrediting Agency, which kicked UGA off the approved list.

Faculty, students, and especially parents were up in arms. Old Gene had gone too far that time. Parents said, "Why should we send our kids and spend our hard-earned money for an education that is not going to be nationally recognized?"

Faculty quietly let the word out that we would not be charged with being absent if we joined the march. A large delegation drove to Atlanta. Idus English and I traveled together. A student leader hung "Ole Gene" in effigy on Tom Watson's statue at the front entrance to the state capitol building in Atlanta. Old Gene's office was directly behind, but he was not in sight. Photographers were swarming all over the place and in fact the story was well publicized in Life magazine. Idus wanted to hide behind a tree because his father was a member of the Georgia General Assembly and Idus did not want Ole Gene's wrath to descend on his dad because he was in the march.

I think this event led to Gene's demise and the rise of Ellis Arnall, who became a reform governor. The Supreme Court's decision on "One Man, One Vote" and outlawing Georgia's infamous county unit system also led to the demise of the Talmadge faction. Under the county unit system, Fulton County had only six votes in the governor's election. The smallest counties had at least two votes regardless of how small they were. Thus the small rural counties in Georgia always held control of the governor's office.

Idus English invited me to go with him to the Athens airport for my first airplane ride on December 7th, 1941. Idus had completed enough training and flying time to enable him to carry a passenger. We flew around Athens on that bright December Sunday afternoon for a time. When we landed the plane we were surprised to find no one around the planes. We entered the hangar and discovered everyone was standing around and listening to the radio. Pearl Harbor had been bombed and we knew that the USA soon would be at war!

In fact, the peace-time draft was underway before Pearl Harbor, as I recall. I know that while hitchhiking back to Athens one Sunday I was picked up by a group of men headed for Fort Jackson, SC. They either had been drafted or were reserves that had been called to active duty. They were not happy.

But we knew that war clouds had been gathering. The Civil Air Patrol at UGA was a government-sponsored training program that gave an early start for pilots who later served in WWII. War had been underway in Europe for a couple of years and it seemed only a matter of time before we in the USA would enter the conflict.

I dropped out of the University of Georgia, not because of the war, but because I had no more money.

# Selling Bibles in North Carolina

## Summer of 1941

After over half a century it is still quite a story that stays in my memory. My father gave me only a few hundred dollars in the fall of 1940 after my summer's work in the Fair Oaks filling station. I went off to the university in Athens for my freshman year. With that money, plus a small 4-H scholarship and a National Youth Administration job in the spring of 1941, I was able to make it through my first year of college.

For my second year, no funds were available. Some students had sold Bibles in prior years for the Southwestern Publishing Company in Nashville, Tennessee. The students who returned for a second or third year and recruited other students got a commission on the Bibles they sold plus a commission on the Bibles sold by the students they had recruited. It sounded pretty good to me and I signed up with a boy named Roy Steadham from Bainbridge, GA. I understand Roy was killed in World War II.

We hitchhiked to Nashville, Tennessee for a few days of orientation and pep talks and instructions on how to sell. Our meetings were held at the company headquarters. We learned such selling techniques as, "If the customer says, 'Salesmen are all a bunch of crooks!' you look the customer straight in the eye and reply, 'Do I look like a crook to you?'" I suppose we did some role playing.

They taught us how to go a week on one change of clothes. There was room in our sample case for a handkerchief and a change of summer underwear. The sample case was well-constructed with metal on every corner. We were instructed not to be scared of dogs but to always face them and move toward them, not away from them. But if we should be attacked, hit them with the sample case.

The sample case contained the book covers and several pages of each book we sold, but not the complete book. We had one of the big family Bibles with pages for the family record and vital statistics. We were instructed to ask each family if they had a Bible. If they did not, it gave us a great opening to show them our sample family Bible and try to sell one. It was our largest Bible, cost the most, and gave us the most profit.

If they had a family Bible we asked if we could see it. In most cases they had to hunt for it and it was usually covered with dust. This gave us a clue as to how interested they were in the Bible, Bible reading, family tree, and so forth. If they had several Bibles we tried to sell them a concordance, Bible dictionary or Bible fact finder. We also had a Bible storybook for children and a book we called a doctor's book with home remedies and drawings of the male and female anatomy.

We tried to get a down payment with each order, even if it was as little as 25 cents. We knew, the bigger the down payment, the more likely customers would be to pay when their book was delivered in the fall. Also, the down payment was used for our living expenses. If no down payment, we had no way to pay our board at the rooming house in town where we stayed on the weekends.

Usually during the week, someone would invite us to have dinner with them and in the evening, supper and a place to spend the night. If no one invited us in to spend the night, we were to find a country church and sleep in it, as country churches were seldom locked. I only recall spending one night sleeping on the hard, wooden benches that were used for pews. On that occasion, I went from noon one day until late the following day with nothing to eat. I suppose that's the longest I have gone in my entire life without any food.

We did not have a car, but walked from house to house. We had hitchhiked from Nashville after attending the Grand Ole Opry on Saturday night. We spent a night in a hotel in Asheville, NC, and finally arrived in Louisburg, NC, a small town north of Raleigh and not far from the Virginia state line.

We did not do well there and Roy said we should go down to Lumberton in Robeson County, NC. Lumberton was in the heart of tobacco-growing country and populated with a mix of whites, blacks, Indians and a fourth group called "Smileys." I suppose Smileys were a mix of the other three groups. At that time, there were four separate school systems in the county to accommodate the four groups.

I spent most of my time with the Indians and learned a great deal from them, enough that I believe some of them were in fact descendants of the famous Lost Colony of 16th century Roanoke Island. Some of the more common names were: Sampson, Oxendine, Locklear, and Jones. Growing tobacco was their main crop and my goal was to sell, take orders, and deliver in the fall when the tobacco was sold. We saw men, women, and children working their crops. From June to September, plowing, suckering (pulling off the side shoots), pulling the leaves from the stalks, and putting them on a small wooden sled that was pulled between the rows by a horse. At some point, the leaves were tied together, placed on wooden poles and placed row-on-row to the top of the tobacco barn.

Then the tobacco was cured by heat from a fire, day and night for quite a number of hours. The leaves eventually turned a golden yellow and were ready to be placed on a flat tobacco basket to be taken to the tobacco warehouse for sale at auction. Tobacco is probably the most labor intensive of all crops. Seed beds were started in late November or December, covered in event of a severe cold spell and given continuous attention until the following fall – a good nine or ten months of labor.

Most of the farmers were sharecroppers and had to give part of the crop to the landlord. It was a very hard life. Generally, I found tobacco farmers to be decent, hard-working hospitable and religious people. I remember arriving late at night at a home well after dark, and being invited to spend the night. The man then invited me to go down to the river with him to bathe. He lit a torch of pine fat-lighter to use for a lantern.

We returned and went to bed. When I awoke the next morning, I discovered we were in a one room house and all three of us had slept in the same room. Often a family would get up well before daylight, kill a chicken, and serve me fried chicken for breakfast.

Not only were the people hospitable but they knew their neighbors. I always asked who lived in the next two or three houses down the road. Almost without exception, I found out as much or more about the family than I really wanted to know, and much more than the next family would want me to know about themselves.

For example, I had been hearing for a day or two about an elderly couple some distance down the road who had three sons in jail for murder, and each one for a separate murder. I arrived at that home late in the day and was immediately invited to spend the night. The couple must have been in their 70s. The old man went out to milk the cow while the woman prepared supper.

While she prepared the meal, she started talking about her youngest son, the one who may have been her favorite. Then she started talking about the fight. She described it as though she were present at the event. She said, "He took out his knife and cut him." With that she reached in her apron pocket and pulled out a switch blade knife and in a rather angry tone flashed the knife and said, "And this is the knife he cut him with." She still possessed the murder weapon. We had the blessing at mealtime and I believe we read the Bible before bedtime. This was a very religious couple!

Another man I visited at some kind of roadhouse, though he did not invite me to spend the night, had a reputation for being a very mean man. I don't remember exactly why, except possibly he had been accused of keeping a stable of prostitutes. He immediately said he wanted a Bible that was complete, one that included all of "the lost books of the Bible." He insisted that there were more books than in the Apocrypha. I showed him that I had a Bible that included the Apocrypha, but he insisted that there were others.

Another person that I heard about long before I arrived at her home was a woman who had a crazy son. The woman was in her late 40s or 50s and was a very warm, friendly person who invited me to have a Coca Cola and some cake on this hot summer morning. As we talked, she began to show me her photo album with pictures of her child, all in girls' dresses.

As we talked, I kept hearing noises in the next room. Finally, he came out. He was a full grown man in a dress. He had hairy legs sticking out below his knee-length dress. His speech was a babble, but a friendly type. The neighbors had told me that the woman had wanted a girl. When a boy was born, she simply dressed him as a girl and since he was crazy, he did not mind.

But I wondered, who was the craziest? She, at least, did not put her son/daughter in a mental hospital. I continue to wonder what ever happened to him. Did the child outlive the mother? Was he eventually freed of wearing womens' clothes? The neighbors recognized this crazy family but accepted it, as they were completely harmless.

Other families were not so hospitable. One very hot Fourth of July, I came to a house with a lot of people visiting on the front porch. I opened the gate and began to move toward the house. A mean, growling police dog approached me. I remembered my instructions from back in Nashville and did not back off. Nor did the people call off their dog. The dog gradually retreated but continued to growl and bark. I went up to the folks on the porch but was unsuccessful in selling any books.

As I prepared to leave, someone said to me, "You are the only stranger who ever came into this yard that the dog did not bite." I immediately flashed back, "Yes, and I will tell you something else. If that dog had bit me, I would be the last person he would ever bite." I was fully prepared to split that dog's skull with my brief case if it had attacked me. Apparently, the dog sensed that it was in more danger than I was.

The Indians told me a lot about their history. How they were unwilling to fight the white man's war during the Civil War. When the militia came to take the males off to war, the men simply fled far back into the swamps. The women knew how to find them and cared for them as necessary.

Another story was about a very mean, violent, God-hating man who cursed a lot. Then came the Charleston, South Carolina, earthquake and as the earth trembled, the mean man became the man who prayed the loudest of all.

On one occasion, I met an Indian woman and her three beautiful Indian daughters. They were all shelling peas as I came up. The woman was tight-lipped and sullen. She paid little attention to my sales pitch and finally said, "All salesmen are a bunch of crooks." I remembered my sales line and looked her straight in the eye and said, "Lady, do I look like a crook to you?" Immediately she shot back, "Yes, you do! You are as crooked as a blacksnake." With that, she got up and went into the house.

I then turned to the three beautiful daughters and asked what was the problem with their mother. They proceeded to tell me that their father had died only recently. A picture salesman came by and offered to make an enlargement of her husband's most recent and best photo for $3. She accepted his offer. However, when the picture came back it was in a frame. The picture was still $3 but the frame was $17 for a total $20 and no picture without the frame. The poor woman did not have $20, and I was the next salesman to come by.

My most memorable experience and the longest lasting relationship resulted from an event that occurred late one afternoon as I was crossing the railroad tracks in Pembroke, N. C. A man in a pickup truck stopped and asked me if I was the preacher. When I explained who I was and what I was doing, he invited me to come home with him, spend the night, and attend the revival services with him and his family. He further invited me to spend each night with him, go out in a different direction each day from Pembroke and come back each evening to spend the night and go to church with him. I accepted his kind invitation.

Later that evening and the following days, I learned much about that man, Walter Pinchbeck. Walter told me his story. He was not a Lumbee Indian but a Cree Indian. He said that he came across the south as a hobo during the Great Depression of the early 1930s. He traveled by train and in boxcars. When he arrived on a train in Pembroke and saw all the Indians he decided to stay a while. He ended up spending the rest of his life in Pembroke. He was working as Superintendent of Grounds at the Pembroke

College when I met him. He was also very active as a Boy Scout leader working with the Indian boys in the area. He later won the highest award given to Scout Leaders, the Silver Beaver award.

Many years later, Clarice and I were traveling to the Outer Banks of North Carolina and stopped by to see Walter. Walter was not at home but at a nearby Boy Scout meeting. I asked Mrs. Pinchbeck why they were willing to take me, a total stranger into their home and entertain me for a week. I said I certainly would not do that in Atlanta. Her reply was simple and straightforward, "Well, you weren't nothing but a kid." They had seen me as I was and not as I *thought* I was.

I looked up Walter with his scout troop. His passion not only was teaching Indian boys scouting, but moreover something of their heritage and history as Indians. Walter proceeded to give me a hand-painted wood carving of an Indian in full head dress and wrote an inscription to me on the back. I still have it and treasure it.

One day, as I was walking through the country, I saw a farmer plowing his tobacco field. I stopped and waited for him to return to my end of the field. When he returned, he stopped and we talked for a while. As we talked, I kept hearing a buzzing in the tall grass where we were standing. At first I thought it was a buzzing bumble bee, and I looked to see why it did not seem to be moving. Suddenly, as I looked down I was eyeball to eyeball with a rattlesnake. I suppose that was the most frightening moment of my entire lifetime. I think that I jumped straight up three feet and three feet to one side in one movement, which is impossible. But I surely tried. We then looked again for the rattlesnake, but were unable to find it, as he had escaped into the tall grass.

One of my more pleasurable evenings was spent in the home of a family with three teenaged daughters. It was a very warm and friendly family. Imagine, a family with three good-looking teenaged daughters and inviting a teenaged stranger into their home to spend the night. I was attracted to the redhead and I think we exchanged letters for a time. She planned to go to Flora McDonald College nearby.

The Southwestern Publishing Company always had the best of the deal. We had to pay freight and all shipping costs in getting the books to us in the fall and had to pay return shipping expenses on books that we could not deliver. Books unsold one year could be sold the next year by the company. As I recall, their offices in Nashville were more like a warehouse, nothing fancy. I have often wondered if they are still in business. I guess, only if they are able to recruit sales people.

I remember we received a sales letter each week listing all salesmen with their sales record. The top salesman with the highest number of sales was listed first and down to the salesman with the least number of sales. I always wondered why Aubrey Lee Malone (I think that was his name) could sell so many more than anyone else. Later I believe that man became quite wealthy in the grocery business in Texas.

I learned that I was not cut out to be a salesman. I have often said that I would not take a thousand dollars for the experience, but would not do it again for a million. I made only enough money to pay for one quarter of college for the fall of 1941.

# Vero Beach, Tampa, and Atlanta

## 1942-1943

After about six weeks of training at the National Youth Administration (NYA) radio school in Marietta, located in a quonset hut building near the Marietta High School, I was offered a job with the U.S. Civil Aeronautics Administration (CAA) working as a radio and teletype operator.

My first assignment was Vero Beach, Florida, where I was to work the graveyard shift from midnight until 8:00 AM. But first, I had to learn how to use the teletype machine, how to make a weather report, read the barometer and rain gage, measure cloud height from the ground, and read perforated tape.

Mr. Garrison was station manager, an old navy man who used coarse language, but really was a very fine man. Clarice and I visited him on a trip to Miami some ten years later. The station was used jointly as airport ticket office and a reception area in a small wooden building that seemed to serve the purpose. Eastern Airlines was the only airline serving Vero Beach at the time and that was only because a man by the name of Bud Holman, a prominent orange grower, was a personal friend of Captain Eddie Rickenbacker, president of Eastern Airlines.

I was to rent a room in the town's only boarding house, a home owned and operated by a very large woman by the name of Ma Hogan. Meals were served family style and there was quite a cross section of boarders there at the time. In addition to Mr. Hogan and their adult daughter, I remember a crew of men from Newnan, GA, that were putting up a water tank, and later, a crew of surveyors that were working at the airport as it was shortly to be turned into a Navy training air base. I also remember a Mr. Wise and the "Bee Man" who took his bees to Florida in winter to work in the fields and orange groves. In the spring, summer, and late fall he took them to the North and Midwest, so the bees could make honey all year.

The water tank crew worked with Cole Construction Company, a hard-working, hard-drinking bunch that worked in summer months inside steel tanks that must have been far over 100 degrees. They made good money and spent it freely. One weekend, two of them got in a knife fight and one was arrested. I don't think anything came of it as both were soon back on the job. I remember them talking about how hot it was painting the inside of the steel tank on a hot Florida summer day.

Years later, one of the same crew members with the same company erected a water tank in Monticello when we lived there, only this time the one crew member I remembered did not work in the tank but operated the lift to pull parts up to the top of the tower for the tank. The survey crew once brought in a very large rattlesnake they had killed. They had cut it open for the skin and found a full-grown rabbit inside.

My most memorable experience at Vero Beach was turning on the airport runway lights for three B-17s. They had to seek an alternate airport after their home field was closed in because of ground fog. I gave them radio instructions but the wind was calm so they could land in any direction. They parked near the station and one got off the runway to park and got stuck in the soft sand. They were all safe and in a very short time our station was also socked in with ground fog.

When the Navy took over the airport, a new terminal was built on the opposite side of the field, but that was after I had moved on for a promotion with slightly better pay at Tampa.

As the war was well underway in mid 1942, personnel were quite fluid. As new employees came on board, they were assigned to the graveyard shift and I was moved up to the evening watch. A new man Dusty Rhodes came in. Once he left the secret blackout instructions assigned to him on top of his desk when he left work. The instructions were for turning off all airport lights and all airway beacons in our area in the event of an enemy attack.

To play a joke on Dusty, I wrote on his set of instructions, "Der Führer will enjoy this," thinking that Rhodes would be more careful next time about leaving secret instructions in the open. Dusty was soon transferred to another state and I was assigned to Tampa.

A few weeks later the joke backfired on me. After I arrived in Tampa, I had a phone call from Mr. Garrison. He was quite upset and asked me if I knew anything about the Hitler writing on Rhodes' file. I readily admitted that I wrote it and told him why I wrote it. It seems that when Rhodes was transferred, his file was sent to the regional office in Atlanta. Someone up there read it and immediately thought, "A spy has infiltrated our operation."

Later the FBI was in Marietta asking questions of Roy McClesky about me. McClesky was the Pure Oil distributor. But I never heard any more about the affair and was eventually transferred to Atlanta from Tampa.

## Vero Beach, Tampa, and Atlanta

One or two other thoughts about Vero Beach in 1942. On my way to the beach I noted a lot of paved streets with light poles out in the jungle. There were no houses on these streets, in fact the jungle seems to have grown up and consumed them. These were the ghosts of the Florida land boom speculation that started after World War I around 1920. No doubt, a lot of people lost a lot of money in these land speculation ventures.

Tampa was a new experience. It was a much larger city, a port city with lots of military activity. McDill field was nearby with B-26 "flying coffin" bomber crews training there. Tampa University, Plant City Park, Ybor City, First Baptist Church and theatres were nearby. Again, I found a room to rent and continued to ride my bicycle to and from work. My work was at Peter O. Knight Airport located at the very end of Davis Island. The bike ride was pleasant, with many fine homes along the way. Next door to the boarding house was a funeral parlor and people from the funeral home frequently ate at the boarding house.

There I met a woman who invited me to visit the Baptist church and then I met a young girl who had recently moved from Atlanta. She seemed pleased to meet someone from Atlanta area and we dated several times. I guess we went to the movies. I know we did not go out to eat as my salary, after paying board and room, did not leave a lot of extra money. My salary increased from $1,200 a year, to $1,440 a year when I left Atlanta for the Air Force at the end of 1943.

Duties at the Tampa airport were actually less than at Vero Beach, as this station had a full time U.S. Weather Bureau staff to make all weather observations. The weather reporter simply handed me the hourly report and I in turn punched up the tape and put it on the teletype machine.

One woman on the night shift, a young girl I should add, talked a lot. One night she asked me to marry her, then asked me to ask her to marry me. At any rate, I refused both offers. She slept on the counter in her office between hourly weather observations, but I never had to wake her up and I don't think she ever missed a sequence.

One night some weather reporter incorrectly reported snow in south Florida. That created quite a few comments up and down the teletype line.

There were some 30 to 50 stations on each teletype circuit. In Atlanta one circuit was Chicago-Atlanta-Miami. Another was Dallas-Ft. Worth-New Orleans-Atlanta-Miami, and a third was on the east coast, Boston-New York-Washington DC-Atlanta-Miami, with Atlanta being the switching station between the three circuits.

With so many big stations and much smaller stations in between, staff would occasionally become bored during the graveyard hours and enter nonsense on their machines. This was strictly forbidden but at 2 or 3 AM on a clear quiet night, it was overlooked. Sometimes two, three, or four operators would enter the dialogue.

Severe weather was a different story. Five bells on the machine interrupted the usual flow of weather and sometimes a station would have to file two or three reports in addition to their regular hourly reports.

Shortly after arriving at Tampa, I again filed for a promotion. The fastest way to get a promotion was to file "any," meaning that one was ready and willing to go anywhere in the USA or Alaska where the CAA operated, so long as there was a promotion and an increase in salary. Thus, sometime in early 1943 I was promoted and back in Atlanta.

I boarded with a Mrs. Robinson on Virginia Avenue and my roommate was Alec Darby, a top mechanic with Delta airlines. One night Alec was riding in the back seat of a car that was involved in an accident and he suffered a severe head injury. He had to have a steel plate put in his head. That kept him out of the draft, but he became one of Delta's chief mechanics.

Working at the Atlanta airport was the best of all possible assignments. It was a big station with several staff on duty at all times. No longer did I work alone on the graveyard shift. As I have noted, Atlanta had the responsibility of collecting all tape on each of the three circuits and starting about 45 minutes after the hour, filing the hourly reports at 30 minutes past the hour, and relaying reports from circuit A to B and C; from C to B and A and from B to A and C circuits.

It was also necessary for Atlanta to enter its report on all three circuits in its assigned sequence. Usually one worked no more than four hours at this position, and then switched to take over the air traffic report and giving weather reports to aircraft flying over or near Atlanta but not landing in Atlanta.

Atlanta also had one other interesting responsibility. That was to give a "time tick" at midnight and again at 12 noon. This action took priority over all other traffic. All stations on the circuits had to be synchronized to the second. Otherwise, reports from two or more stations could be entered at the same time and messages would be garbled up with no traffic getting through. Time checks were a vital function of each station on each circuit.

The Atlanta operator at five minutes to noon and midnight would have a radio tuned to Ft. Collins, or some other assigned station, that broadcast a continuous time signal. Once the master clock was set (usually it seldom varied more than one or two seconds), Atlanta was then ready to interrupt all traffic on the three circuits and sound the bell on all three circuits precisely at noon and midnight.

With days off, I was able to go by trackless trolley into downtown Atlanta and go by trolley to Marietta and home for a few hours, climb Kennesaw Mountain with Pauline, or whatever.

At Thanksgiving, I helped unload boxcars for the Georgia Baptist Children's home at Hapeville. It was always interesting to open a boxcar because we never knew what would be in it: clothing, canned goods, or hay and feed for livestock.

Mrs. Douglas Davis was Sunday School teacher for young adults at the Hapeville Baptist Church. She was a fine lady, with some old fashioned, ultra-conservative ideas, but still a fine lady. She entertained in her home and on one occasion asked me to teach her daughter to drive. I made the mistake of allowing her brother Doug to ride along in the back seat. His running comments and criticism of Darlene unnerved her and she turned around from the driver's seat and chewed her brother out. I had to grab the steering wheel.

Doug was a very creative person, a budding artist who later attended the School of Art at the University of Georgia, where he met Joe Perrin, who later became head of the Art department at Georgia State University in Atlanta and later Clarice's art teacher.

Doug moved to Paris after the war and was bringing home a lot of his paintings to Atlanta with a plane load of Atlanta's best known art patrons. The plane was attempting to take off from Orly Field in Paris and must have been heavily overloaded. All passengers were killed. I learned from Mrs. Davis that Doug was on the plane and that a friend of Doug's phoned Mrs. Davis to tell her that Doug had asked each of the patrons to carry one of his paintings on board. It was a quick and easy way for Doug to get a lot of his work home. I am sure the rest of the art patrons were attempting to bring home a lot of art they had collected in Paris.

The people of Paris gave Auguste Rodin's sculpture "The Shade" to Atlanta and it now stands near an entrance of Atlanta's High Museum of Art as a memorial to the Atlantans killed in the Orly plane crash.

In Mrs. Davis' Sunday School class, I met Dorothy and Florence Thrailkill. They frequently invited me into their home for Sunday dinner and I was glad to accept. Their mother was a fine cook. Forrest Gerrard was also a member of the class. He later became a pastor and for years was assistant pastor of the Smyrna First Baptist Church.

So my time in Atlanta passed very quickly and then came my draft notice. I had announced on more than one occasion that I planned to enlist in the Army Air Force, but was asked by the regional director B. L. Weinberg to continue on with the CAA, as my position was considered critical to the defense effort. However, the local draft board in Vero Beach where I first registered thought otherwise. With a notice to appear for induction, I knew it was time to seek out the Army Air Force recruiting office. It was in the Post Office building in downtown Atlanta and I was sworn in the latter part of December 1943. My discharge papers say December 31, 1943, but I believe I was sworn in several days before that date.

Francis on Kennesaw Mountain in 1942, taking a break from radio school in Marietta.

# War

## U.S. Army Air Force
## Dec. 1943 - 1946 (2 years, 4 months, 8 days)

I enlisted in the Army Air Force with dreams of becoming a pilot after NYA radio school training and the years when I served with the Civil Aeronautics Administration as a radio and teletype operator.

Francis, Army Air Force, 1945

My first days of military service were spent at Fort McPherson in Atlanta. First were the usual physical exam and shots to prevent diseases. I well remember the wall cartoon located just before going into the shot room. A doctor with a patch on one eye with a bloody apron and holding a very large fly-spray gun-size syringe with a forked needle. I am sure it helped the nearly naked inductees to laugh and relieve some of the tension.

However, as we went through the shot line a medical technician was on either side of the line of inductees to give a shot in each arm. The man in front of me suddenly slumped and fainted. I stopped and immediately I received two more shots! The technicians were so mechanical they had simply put down one set of syringes, picked up another set and whipped around to the next set of arms, except mine were the same set. I did not wait for the third round of shots but stepped over the collapsed body in front of me.

Travel was by train from the old Union Station railroad terminal on Forsyth Street in downtown Atlanta to basic training in Keesler Field in Mississippi. In the USA travel was by train, but later I was to travel by ship and air before I was discharged.

Keesler Field was a crowded place with thousands of raw recruits. A few from Atlanta and the South were to be with me all the way to Italy. "Smokey" Whaley from Gatlinburg, TN, was a very memorable person. At early morning roll call (way before dawn) Smokey would be laughing and dancing. Of the hundreds of inductees, he seemed to be the only one in a cheerful mood at that ungodly hour.

Morgan McNeil III, son of the president of McNeil Marble Company in Marietta was a pleasant young man. Perhaps because he was somewhat smaller than most of us, he was sent directly from basic training to gunnery school and then overseas to England. He was killed when his bomber was shot down over Europe.

William Tyndale was with me all the way through basic training, radio school, gunnery school, Goldsboro, NC, and Falconera, Italy. William came home, married, and then both he and his wife contracted polio and both were paralyzed from the waist down and immobile except for the use of their wheel chairs. Their father was a fairly wealthy man and constructed their homes to provide maximum mobility. Later both committed suicide.

Frank Mason of Atlanta and Tommy Tacker from Humboldt, TN, were with me all the way. Tommy and I continued to correspond for several years after the war and I had hoped to visit him but never have.

Keesler Field was a crowded, busy place. Drilling and KP (kitchen police, kitchen duty) come to mind. I had received plenty of drilling in ROTC at Athens, so that was no big deal. KP was something else. On KP detail we were awakened around 2 AM to dress and go down to the kitchen to prepare breakfast. Whole 30 dozen egg cases were brought in and eggs were cracked into huge vats. With so many eggs to crack it was not surprising that bits and pieces of egg shell got mixed into the scrambled eggs.

Once I was assigned to coffee-making detail. The coffee was placed into a large bag before going into the coffee urn. I asked the cook for a string to tie the coffee bag. He promptly reached for an old dirty mop, pulled out his pocket knife and cut a mop string and handed it to me. This I used to tie the coffee bag. The cook assured me that since the coffee was to be boiled, it was OK to use a dirty mop string.

On another occasion, William Tyndale was eating a bowl of oatmeal for breakfast when he suddenly spit out a big lump of octagon soap. I suppose the cook felt a little lump of soap in the oatmeal would never be noticed.

Other than the long KP days, I remember little about Keesler Field, It was early spring when we left Keesler Field on a troop train for Sioux Falls, South Dakota. I don't know how long it took to make the trip but it seems we traveled by way of Chicago and I know up to Minneapolis, Minnesota. I remember the good women of Minneapolis serving us a wonderful breakfast at the train station.

When we arrived in Sioux Falls on May $2^{nd}$, it was still winter with eight inches of snow on the ground. Quite a change from Mississippi and it was back into winter clothes. There were long weeks of training in radio, voice, code, radio theory, and mechanics – spring, summer and into early fall. We also had PT and first flight in a small trainer using radio equipment. We lived in tar paper-covered barracks heated with coal stoves.

I did have some free weekends and made several trips out to Iowa by hitchhiking. A great time to visit the Oppedals, Eugene O'Neal, and Uncle Bill, Aunt Edith and Marvin. Marvin and I went out hunting one afternoon but the ragweeds were as high as my head and full of pollen. I was immediately overcome with hay fever: eyes running, nose running, itching and sneezing so bad I thought I might not even be able to get back to the house. I even had a hard time breathing. This was the worst case of hay fever I ever had.

I did attend the First Baptist Church in Sioux Falls, SD. It was there that I was baptized. The pastor wanted me to wear my uniform for the service and I did. I believe his name was Augustus M. Hintz. I had joined the Baptist church when I was a student at the University of Georgia, but was never baptized. Why, I do not know, except I was never notified as to the date for the service.

The time passed quickly with no time for sightseeing during wartime, but I am not sure there was much to see other than farms in that section of the USA. Anyway, it was soon time to leave Sioux Falls. We left in the fall, and again, we were back in winter clothes.

From Sioux Falls we went east by troop train (not southwest toward Yuma, AZ.) to Esterville, IA. At some point, we turned and headed west but I do not remember the route. When we got to Yuma it was summertime again, although the calendar said fall. We arrived in winter clothes late at night but it was very hot. Our winter wool clothes were much too hot and sticky and soon we were back in summer clothes again. In Yuma we lived in tents and on a wooden platform.

Our commanding officer was a West Point graduate who wanted to make the place look like a resort. (Imagine a resort area with only tents to live in.) Anyway, he managed to bring in hundreds of huge palm trees to line the streets. One day he made a command decision to trim the palm trees and I was one chosen to help trim the trees. We were given old, rusty saws and told to trim the limbs. It would have been an easy task with the right tools and if we were wearing heavy leather gloves, but we had neither. As a result, we did not accomplish much, except bruised and bloody knuckles for our efforts.

We did a lot of practice with machine guns, shotguns, and target practice. Practice both on the ground and from the waist gun position while flying in a B-17 bomber. The target was a long sleeve towed by another B-17 as I recall. Later we were to have an experience flying at high altitude and wearing sheep skin wool trousers, jacket, boots and a leather helmet. However, before that we were to learn the importance of wearing our oxygen masks in high-altitude flying.

We were placed about a dozen at a time in a tube-shaped chamber, given pencil and paper, and then told to transcribe Morse code from our head sets. I thought I was doing OK and received instructions to sign my name. The next thing I remember, I was awakened and shortly told to look at my code copy. My last line was simply that, a line across the page from near top to bottom. This was proof positive that our mind plays tricks on us when we lose oxygen. We think we are rational when, in fact, we are passing out. After passing out, an oxygen mask was immediately put on me. We learned that when we lose oxygen, we are not aware of it.

After the high-altitude flight when we wore our oxygen masks, the barracks was very quiet. The flight had been a very exhausting experience for the entire barracks that day and all went immediately to bed to rest.

Skeet shooting at a "clay pigeon" was excellent training in teaching us how to lead our target and swing our weapon at the same time. Once a group of us were assigned to clean up a skeet-shooting area. I think our main duty was to pick up all empty shotgun shells. The shooting range was some distance from the camp and we were hauled out in a truck. It did not take long to do the work and we had dead time waiting for our ride back to camp. So, we amused ourselves by slinging out the clay discs and attempting to hit them with rocks. Sometimes we would sling the clay discs out from both sides of the shed at the same time. We managed to waste quite a few of them before the sergeant drove up in the truck and caught us in the act. He threatened to keep us on KP the balance of time we were in Yuma but nothing came of it.

One Sunday, a few of us made a brief trip down into Old Mexico. An American tourist, a Republican, was singing the praises of Tom Dewey. Charles Strible in our group became quite drunk on Mexican beer and wore a big sombrero back to camp. On another occasion, we visited the old territorial prison at Yuma, AZ, and saw a few of the prairie schooners (wagons) used by the pioneers on their treks west.

At first the hot, dry desert was depressing, as it was and is a vast contrast to Iowa farm land or Georgia's red hills and trees. However, by the time we left Yuma in early winter I had become enchanted by the beauty of the land, especially at sunrise and sunset.

Another long troop train brought us all the way across the USA. It seemed that we spent two days simply crossing Texas. Finally, we arrived at Seymour Johnson Field near Goldsboro, NC. This was the site of our real crew training in the two-engine B-25 bombers, also called Billy Mitchells for a pioneer military aviator. Modified versions of the B-25 were used to fly from an aircraft carrier, bomb Japan, and then fly on to China.

Night flying, radio operating, to give our flight position, and more gunnery training. We were assigned to wooden barracks and we were into winter weather flying. Long hours of waiting in the hangar for takeoff time. It was there that I first drank black coffee as that was all we had. It did not taste good, but I suppose it was to keep us awake. Also, the coffee helped in some way to kill time.

On one night flight, we flew out over the Gulf of Mexico. In reporting our position back to Seymour Johnson, there were times when we were unable to make contact. I would then broadcast to "any army radio." A station in the far west USA would come in loud and clear and I would report our position.

However, because of army relay delays we would sometimes be back on the ground at the field before our position report arrived. As a result, we were told not to broadcast to "any army radio" again, only to our base station.

As Easter approached we were headed for an Eastern seaport and on Easter Sunday, 1945, we were at Camp Patrick Henry, near Norfolk, Virginia, and ready to board ship for Europe. We did not know where in Europe. On the appointed night we boarded the USS West Point, the former USS America, the largest American liner at that time.

We were to travel unescorted across the Atlantic. It was quite an adventure. Bunks were stacked four high and were folded up against the wall (bulkheads, I believe was the navy term) during the non-sleeping hours and we were very crowded. Meals were served at all kinds of crazy hours and we were served at very narrow tables where we stood to eat. There was no such luxury as eating sitting down in comfortable chairs.

We had been at sea only a very short time when we heard that our president Franklin Roosevelt had died at Warm Springs, GA. I don't know of any special memorial services, and besides, there were probably several thousand of us on the ship.

Some of us did have a rather unique opportunity for entertainment. Red Skelton was on board the ship and on one of the upper decks he entertained us. It so happens that this deck was reserved at the time for officers. However, we enlisted airmen got around it by wearing our flight uniforms that were the same as those of the officers and without any insignia of rank showing. Thus, the ship patrol officers let us up. Red was doing his baby-bathing and diaper-changing routine and that kept us laughing.

One other very memorable event was a storm at sea. With the ship constantly rolling and pitching, I along with many others became seasick and headed for the ship's rail to heave up. Unfortunately, we heaved into the wind and the upchuck came back on us. Next time we went to the ship rail away from the wind.

I had purchased some barber tools and volunteered to cut hair. I gave William Tyndale a GI haircut and that was about the extent of my barbering, as I sold the clippers shortly after we reached Italy.

As we approached the Straits of Gibraltar, PBY flying boats (patrol boats) were out to escort us. Later blimps were to escort us through the straits and into the Mediterranean Sea. The big rock flashed signals at a very rapid rate. By morning we were docking in Naples, Italy.

A long line of beggars were lined up as we walked off the gangplank and onto solid ground. At the end of the line of beggars and on his knees with his cap in his hand to receive coins, we saw a familiar face. We all laughed as we recognized Red Skelton.

We were loaded into open trucks to travel through Naples. Some tossed out candy bars to the people while others tossed out bars of soap and yelled, "Get a bath you dirty dagos." Not a very nice thing to say to those people, but it was said by some on the truck.

19th Replacement Depot (Repple-Depple), Naples, Italy.

Notes from my WW II photo album: First stop in Italy. Noted for its dust, chilly nights, and terrible food. Arrived 14th April, 1945 on USS West Point. Departed for Falconera, Italy, 21st April in C-47. On our first pass we visit Caserta. Children gathered outside the transient mess hall swamp us when we carry out bread to them. The older boys and men try to sell us cameos and buy cigarettes. We learn about the black market.

Once more, we were assigned to a tent city while awaiting transfer to our assigned air base. With nothing else to do, a couple of us volunteered for garbage-hauling detail. We knew it would give us an opportunity to see some of the city outside the camp. What I remember at the garbage dump was a group of children and perhaps adults fighting over the garbage that we tossed off the truck.

Later, during dinner at the Allied Transient Mess, children standing outside were calling in for us to bring them food. One small boy was seated on a window ledge where he could watch us eat. He called out, "Hey Joe, bring me some bread, bring me some bread." I nodded to him and as I finished my meal carried out part of a loaf of bread to give to the boy. I had to walk through the swarm of children and held my arm up high with the bread. However, a big girl leaped up and snatched the bread from my hand. I shall never forget the sad look on the small boy's face as he watched from his window ledge. His meal had been snatched from him.

Daily we ran into soldiers from all over the world. Besides these South African soldiers, we met Indian, Polish, Canadian, Yugoslav, French, English, Greek, Norwegian, and New Zealand soldiers and sailors.

Falconara, Italy, was my next assignment. The 448$^{th}$ Bomb Squadron, 12$^{th}$ Army Air Force was located very near the Adriatic Sea and was the site of a former airfield and barracks for Italian Air Force cadets.

In Falconara, the enlisted men had the barracks and the officers lived in tents. Quite a switch from the usual. The landing strip was steel mats. The airfield was on a fairly level site between farm houses.

War

In Falconara an old man picks out bits of coal among ashes dropped from railway engine fire boxes.

Bombed-out buildings in Ancona. These houses suffered because they were located within 100 yards of the waterfront.

A few days later, I was able to photograph a group of farmers partaking of their noonday meal, picnic style in the open air. They had been thrashing wheat and seemed to have plenty to eat, including the ever-present bottles of vino.

Italian thrashers at lunch.

The harvest is a very important season in Italy. Practically all the wheat goes into making flour. None of it is wasted, because it takes a lot of bread to feed 45 million people. In Italy the thrashers get bread, macaroni, and vino for supper.

The Italian women took care of our laundry. When I delivered my laundry to a woman at a nearby farmhouse, she first sewed a mark with thread into each item of clothing before washing. So our own socks, shorts, undershirts, and shirts were always returned to us.

The farm dwelling was on the second floor and the ground floor was a stable for horses and cows. However, the pigpen was separate. The floor of the pigpen was concrete and the pig urine flowed into a pit. Odor from the pig urine pit was probably the stinkingest odor I have ever encountered. This urine and manure from the stables was hauled out to fertilize the grape vines. Good farming practice, but I doubt that many folks in the USA know that their Italian vino (wine) was fertilized this way.

One night I had guard duty with two or three planes to guard. The B-25s were parked very near the farmhouses and my watch lasted only about four hours, or so. Nothing to do but keep a loaded 45-caliber pistol in my holster and stand and watch. No walking, no patrolling, just watch, look and listen. Occasionally a military police officer would ride by to check on me.

I was sent up on only one bombing mission. It seems that many airmen were anxious to complete their 25 missions so they could go home and as a result I waited several days after arrival before finally being assigned to a flight. Briefing was held in a very large room with a large map that covered the entire wall of the building. The map showed northern Italy and much of southern Europe. The target was a site in the area of the Brenner Pass. Watches were synchronized.

At the plane, I was given a large camera and told that I was to be a photographer on the mission. I protested that I had never even seen that type of camera before, let alone had any training as to how to use it. I was told that there was nothing to it. The camera was loaded, and all I had to do was pull the camera trigger as fast as I could to take bomb strike photos in the target area. A small round opening was located just under the radio station where I would normally be to operate the radio transmitter.

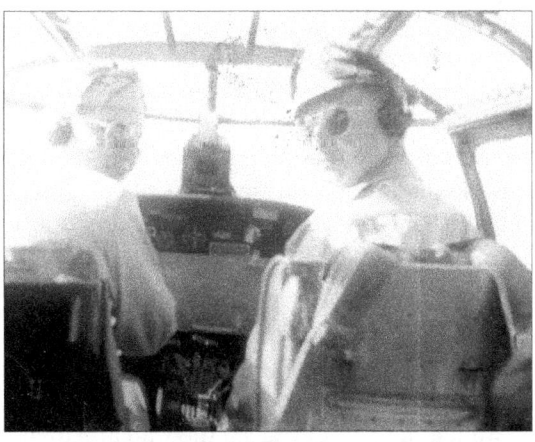

Bomber pilots for the plane I was on.

Out over the Adriatic Sea I test fired both waist machine guns. We were flying in what was called boxes of nine and in a very tight formation. Each group of three was at a slightly different flying level, so as to give maximum fire power against any enemy aircraft and also not to hit one of our own ships.

In addition, we had fighter-plane escorts. Naturally they could fly much faster than could our loaded bombers, but they cut back their throttles to stay near us. However, there was a heavy fog over the area and bombs were not dropped. We returned to base.

This was the last flight of the war for the 448$^{th}$ Bomb Squadron. My discharge papers show that I fought in air combat in the Balkans, Po Valley, and Central Europe. Decorations and citations included American Theatre service medal; AEME (Africa, Europe, Middle East) service medal; three bronze service medals, Good Conduct medal, and World War II Victory medal. I have never seen all those medals and I know there were a lot of folks ahead of me that deserved them a lot more than I did. Anyway, that is what shows up on my discharge papers.

Back to the last mission of the war. When we landed, the crew chief proceeded to chew me out, saying all kinds of nasty things to me. I had not removed the gun covers from the machine guns before the flight and thus I blew holes in both gun covers when I test fired the guns over the Adriatic Sea. No one had told me about the gun covers as we never had any back in the States and besides I was busy fooling with the camera before we took off. Such are my memories of the last flight of the 448$^{th}$ Bomb Squadron in Italy at the end of World War II in Europe.

Celebration of VE day took the form of shooting Vary pistols from one barracks, across the compound yard and to the barracks across the way. Vary pistols were used to shoot flares into the sky at night. I suppose a person in a downed plane could use it to help rescue teams find the location. Soon, a few officers who had the pistols from the planes started shooting at fellow officers' tents. Possibly a few were set afire, I don't recall. The next day all the Vary pistols were taken up.

Latrines in the cadet barracks were something else. A hole in the floor with a slightly raised spot for each foot. When the water tank was flushed, water came down from the tank and covered everything but our shoes. However in the city, latrines for men were completely exposed. Located against an outside wall, a man simply faced the wall and disposed of excess urine from wine, etc. I don't know where the women's "necessaries" were located.

# War

Caption from my Army photo album: Homeward bound!

We had a lot of free time when the war in Europe ended, and we tried to make the best of it. We fully expected first to be shipped to the USA and then across the Pacific for the invasion of Japan.

We flew back to the United States by way of North Africa, Ascension Island in the South Atlantic, and Brazil.

# Mercer

After I was discharged at the end of World War II, I had a very nice scholarship, the GI Bill. This made it possible for me to continue my college education without constant worry about how I was to pay for it. I certainly did not expect any more help from home. Dad still had Dallas, Pauline, and David at home. Dorothy had struck out on her own as soon as she finished high school and likewise, Barbara.

I had pretty much decided to enter the ministry. In part, this decision was a result of seeing first hand some of the aftermaths of the hell of war. Whole cities were laid open from bombing and shelling. I saw thousands of folks fleeing south from war-ravaged northern Italy and children begging for bread and still other folks fighting for the garbage we GIs were throwing out. I saw an old man on his knees picking up tiny bits of coal, along the railroad tracks to be used for fuel at home.

After my entry classification tests at Mercer, my counselor stated that I appeared to be well qualified to study law. However, law had never entered my mind, although I very much liked the study of government at Acworth High School and heard plenty about government from the folks who came into the store. Also, we had a radio and regularly received the *Atlanta Constitution*, the liberal newspaper at the time, and still considered to be the most liberal of the two major papers in Atlanta.

Mercer was quite a contrast to the university in Athens. Mercer was one small campus with only a few hundred students in contrast to the 3,500 at UGA. Classes were smaller and we came to know the names of many of our classmates by their first names as well as the names of our faculty members.

Mercer was a Baptist college that I first learned about while working in Tampa in the early days of WWII and also from my chaplain in Italy.

I joined the choir, attended Baptist Student Union activities, joined the honorary Alpha Phi Omega service fraternity, and later joined the ministerial association. As a result of being a member of the ministerial association, I was elected to serve as their representative to student government.

Classes were much smaller at Mercer and, since I was now on the GI Bill, it was possible for me to go to classes all year: spring, summer, fall and winter quarters. I was in a hurry to get through as it was now the summer of 1946 and I had first started college in the fall of 1940. I was still only a sophomore and, in addition, many of my agriculture classes were not transferable to Mercer. So in a sense, I had to start all over. ROTC credits were not accepted initially, however Mercer later added ROTC and the UGA credits were reinstated.

Classes included a number of mandatory Bible classes, both Old and New Testaments, and chapel once or twice a week. I especially liked church history and managed to major in both English literature and church history. A foreign language was also required and I struggled with Spanish.

One course in education was a breeze. "Bull Shooting" Anthony taught economics. He also spent a lot of time in a booth in the nearby drugstore. He smoked a lot and never shook the ash off his cigarette. Students would guess how long the ash would get before it fell on B. S. Anthony's shirt. He was a sloppy dresser and often used a safety pin to keep his shirttail tucked in. However, it was a delight to hear him lecture. He always called the roll, but never looked up to see who was answering to the roll. On occasion he would announce after completing the roll, "A grand slam this morning!" meaning 100 percent in attendance. Then one or two latecomers would stroll in and he would then announce, "A grand slam plus two this morning."

One summer quarter I had three courses: The Romantic Movement in English Literature, marriage, and astronomy. This was also the summer that I became engaged to my future bride and dear wife-to-be. How could I not get engaged after those three courses? Marriage was delayed only about six months after our engagement.

During my first year and a half at Mercer I roomed on the second floor of Sherwood Hall with three other WWII veterans. Sam Culpepper, Lucius Hall, and Ben Alexander. Lucius was probably the one with the best academic record but a very poor credit risk. He walked with a limp as he had been shot in the leg during the war. Sam was a pleasant, easy-going fellow, quiet, reserved and timid around the girls. Ben Alexander was somewhat of a mystery man because he tended to be a bit suspicious of folks. I learned only later that he kept a pistol with him, even at Mercer.

Sam Culpepper and I once decided to play a joke on Ben, pretending that we were federal undercover agents. We talked in a kind of code that made absolutely no sense but Ben really believed we were federal agents.

Ben dated a girl named Christine Wortham. Her father was manager of the Massey Lane farm south of Macon and near Fort Valley. The owner had a very fine collection of camellias, one of the best in the South. This farm is now the headquarters of the National Camellia Society. Clarice and I were married on December 21, 1947, and Christine supplied the church and the reception area with the finest display of camellias that could be had.

Sam was a rather shy person. He knew that I was dating as many girls as possible and once asked me who would be a girl for him to date. He said he was afraid he might ask a girl who was already spoken for by another man. I then proceeded to prepare a list of ten girls that I thought were not dating anyone regularly. I placed the name of an attractive lady at the top of the list, a girl named Martha Andrews, a girl that I had not gotten around to dating as I was pretty much committed to Clarice by that time.

Sam asked Martha for a date and never dated anyone else, so far as I know. They were married and, from all reports, happily married. Sam became an attorney with a practice in Fort Valley, GA. Unfortunately, Sam died too young.

Lucious Hall attended Crozer Seminary one year ahead of me but did not finish. He owed the seminary money when he left and they confiscated his large collection of books. Before I left the seminary Lucious contacted me and asked if I could rescue his books for him. The dean was willing to let me have them and I brought them back to Georgia when I became pastor at Monticello. Lucious then came to pick up his books. He later married and I never heard from him again, although his wife did write a time or two, telling us that her husband's health was not good. He was director of a Baptist student group out in Oklahoma the last time I heard from him.

Ben Alexander and Christine moved to Ohio. Ben was a mail carrier the last I heard from them.

During most of the year before my marriage, I was into dating, as were most of us on the campus. We walked the girls home from vespers each evening, attended retreats, and one year I was assigned to drive the student activity bus to the Southern Baptist Assembly at Ridgecrest, NC.

But, most of my dating became focused on Clarice. Our mutual friend Faith Daniel introduced us. I first remember meeting Clarice in the campus hangout. Clarice and Faith were in a booth, eating or talking. I thought she was a bit standoffish, a bit different than the others and a bit more mature as she had finished nursing school at Charity Hospital in New Orleans, Louisiana.

At any rate, I asked her for a date and she accepted. Then I asked her for a second date. The girls in the dorm immediately told Clarice, "Francis must be serious about you, Clarice. He has never dated any of us more than once and he has dated quite a number."

Clarice started working at Middle Georgia Hospital on the evening shift. I would frequently meet her at night after she finished work and walk her back to the campus. Once Clarice's friend Faith, her friend Guy Walton, and I planned a surprise birthday celebration for Clarice. They waited about halfway between the hospital and the campus for us to return. They had a small cake and candle and a happy birthday song for her. Both sang well, much better than I. As a matter of fact, Clarice also has a beautiful voice. She took singing lessons for a while at Mercer, but hospital work, class work on her RN degree, and courting me was a big load. She said she would have made better grades if not for working and courting so much. I believe her.

At the time of our wedding, we naturally had our Mercer friends with us for the occasion, male and female. Ray Brewster, Ben Alexander, and I believe, Lucius Hall attended. Ben was to be the official photographer but his camera failed and thus we had no good photos of our wedding. Also, my brother Dallas was in my wedding party. Dallas did not tell me, but he later told Jim Ann than he thought it was much too much. In a sense he was outside the loop, as there was a big gap in our ages and he did not know anyone else in the wedding party.

Being practical jokesters, Ray Brewster and Lucius Hall put soot in my new socks while I was doing something else on the morning of our wedding. Naturally, I was not thinking about my friends doing such a stunt on my wedding day. However, the morning after our wedding night there was lots of soot on our nice, new sheets.

Lewis Poetter and his wife Mable were house parents in Sherwood Hall. Lewis had a peg leg and walked with a decided limp. He asked me to join the service fraternity. The object was to provide various kinds of services on the campus. That sounded good to me, until he suggested that I join in an effort to raise enough money to put a cross on the highest tower of the main building. I had a look at the tower and determined that it was not practical or safe. The project was never started. As our fraternity had the Coke machines on the campus, for a time I collected the money and restocked the machines.

Lewis once made a statement to me that sounded very strange. He said to me, "I never accept anyone until they prove themselves to me on my terms." My immediate reply was, "Lewis, you are going to be a very lonely man."

Later, my statement proved to be prophetic. Lewis obtained a PhD in Psychology and raised enough money to build and staff a large and fully-accredited school for emotionally-disturbed boys, Anneewakee. However, they had to have parents with plenty of money or plenty of insurance. They did not accept poor boys. Lewis took some of the boys on trips to Florida and to Old Mexico. Lewis was later accused and convicted of sexually molesting a number of the boys. Lewis was sent to one of the state correctional facilities at Milledgeville, GA. I am sure he was lonely during his jail time. It is interesting that it was his daughters and not his wife who helped to convict Lewis. So, Mercer, like any other school or college had some that did not turn out too well.

George Fields and his wife Nell became our friends at Mercer and have remained our close friends for over 50 years. George came up to help me with a revival while I was a student pastor of a little country church in Morgan County, Gibbs Memorial Baptist Church. George was to follow me as pastor of that church. George and Nell went to Louisville Seminary after Mercer, but we kept in close contact and continued to be close friends during our pastorates. They are very dear friends to this day.

# Gibbs Memorial Baptist Church

## 1948

Memories can be a bit fuzzy in thinking back over a half century. However, most of my memories of Gibbs Memorial Baptist Church are very pleasant ones. Mr. Homer Echols, a fine old man, said he stayed awake long enough to see that the preacher was starting off OK, and then he drifted off to sleep.

Mr. Hammond Calloway was known as "Mr. Baptist" around the state, as he was very active in his church and in Baptist association matters and regularly attended the annual Georgia Baptist Convention. He was a fine, dedicated Christian gentleman.

When I became pastor at Bostwick, I met WalterRuark's parents. Walter was a University of Georgia friend and a sergeant in ROTC there. Walter was killed in the Battle of the Bulge in WWII. His parents were a fine older couple and showed me a large collection of Walter's football, ROTC, and other mementos.

One of my most memorable experiences was a visit I made to an elderly lady and member who lived in Madison. I had been asked to visit this elderly, sick lady and encourage her to live in the "county home," a nursing home, where she could have a warm room and adequate food and care. She had consistently refused to do so. As a young, enthusiastic preacher, I readily agreed to see the lady. This lady had been active in the church for a number of years and members were very concerned about her well-being.

I visited this lady on a raw, cold, damp winter day. I found her in a bed in the hall as I recall. There was no heat in the building. There was bread and other cold food on the table in the kitchen. The lady said to me, "I know what you are going to say to me before you say it." Naturally, I asked her what that was. She said, "You are going to ask me to go to the county home – and I am not going!"

My instant replay was, "No, I am not going to say that." You see, I had changed my mind as soon as she spoke. Later, while a student in the seminary I was taking a course in pastoral counseling and related that incident to my teacher. I asked him why would a person choose to stay in such misery, when they could have a place that offered shelter, comfort and food. His immediate replay was, "That's easy. She much preferred her freedom and independence to living under someone else's supervision in a county home."

I never forgot the lesson that lady and my instructor taught me. We must respect and honor peoples' choices, no matter how difficult their plight may seem to us.

Our son Lonnie was born while I was pastor at Gibbs Memorial. Not long after, our Gibbs Memorial Church families came to visit us in our basement apartment in Macon and brought us a lot of food. We were both pleased and surprised that folks would drive all the way down to visit us and bring us so much food.

Finally, one other memory. I was given free rein in planning the revival and I elected to have a song leader and a different preacher each night. That meant folks at Gibbs Memorial prepared and served a lot of excellent food during the week. Three I remember who preached that week were George Fields, Vernon Brown, and Tucker Singleton. I don't remember who the others were. Vernon later became pastor of the First Baptist Church in Daytona Beach, FL, and I believe he had a radio ministry in south Alabama for a number of years. Tucker was very active in Georgia Baptist affairs and George Fields followed me as pastor at Gibbs Memorial.

# Crozer Seminary

Crozer Theological Seminary was a vastly different world from Mercer. It was located in upland Pennsylvania, next to Chester on the Delaware River. Chester is an old industrial town with both a Sun Oil company refinery and the Scott Paper Company. It was a working-class town that was drab and dirty in winter. Ship foghorns bellowed on foggy nights.

Crozer had a small student body with less than 50 students in three classes. However, it had a good faculty and a great library.

I had been drawn to Crozer as a result of serving as assistant pastor of the Tattnall Square Baptist Church located on the Mercer campus. The pastor was Dr. Eric Oesterle, a graduate of Crozer and a chaplain who served at Warner Robins Air Base during World War II. Dr. Oesterle was a graduate of Crozer and he recommended the seminary to me and was eager to give me a good reference.

In addition, since I was married and with one son, we needed some type of housing other than a dormitory. So many ex-GI's were going to the Southern Baptist seminaries that they had no housing for married students available. Thus, we chose Crozer. My former roommate, Lucius Hall and another Mercer student, DuPree Jordan both entered Crozer the year earlier, but both dropped out at the end of their first year. Dupree entered the communication field and later established his own business, Jordan Enterprises in Atlanta.

Cary and Florence Gordy, our friends of earlier years, entered Crozer when we did. As they had no children at the time, they lived in Old Main and ate in the dining room. We lived the first year in the former president's home, a very large three-story building, with Wendell and Shirley Malloch. They were from Arkansas.

With such a small student body, most of us were quickly on a first name basis. In my class were Cary Gordy, Raymond Detrich, Fred Stom, Walter Stark, George Lawrence, Myron Cheney, John Mates, and later Stan Hanson. Other students in earlier and later classes were Eugene Drew, Bob Coe, James Greene, Ed Brooks, En Chin Lin, Makoto Sakabarshia, Cyrl

Pyle, Jimmie Biashia, Walter McCall, Martin Luther King, Jr., Ed Spath, Durham Ipock, Joseph Kirkland, John (Jack) Shoemaker, Marcus Wood, William Tasker, Larry Seyler, Lawrence Lutz, Reese Mahoney, Art Dechent, Calixto Marques, and others.

Naturally, classes at Crozer were small with usually no more than a dozen and some as few as five or six students. All professors were in the traditional mode when it came to teaching. The professor was either standing or seated behind the desk. Each professor had his own room where all of his classes were taught with the students listening and taking notes on the lecture. James Prichard, Old Testament and Hebrew; Morton Scott Enslin, New Testament and Greek; George Davis, theology; Robert Keighton, homiletics; R. E. Harkness, church history; Charles Batten, Christian education and Kenneth "Snuffy" Smith, Christian ethics. My two favorites were Harkness and Smith. Harkness because of my love of church history and Smith because he challenged all (both students and faculty) in making our Christianity relevant to the here and now.

Snuffy Smith entered the civil rights struggle in the 50s and 60s all out. He visited and widely publicized the utterly horrible classrooms some of the black Chester students had to use. Some classrooms were in dark, damp basement rooms. He became very active in the local Democratic party and even managed to get himself locked up in the local jail for a brief period and gained lots of publicity for the just cause. Snuffy Smith taught Martin Luther King, Jr., and practiced what M. L. King later preached and practiced.

I suppose this did not sit well with Dr. Morton Scott Enslin, who was an ultraliberal in scriptural interpretation by current Southern Baptist standards, but an ultraconservative when it came to any kind of social action. Once I invited Dr. Clarence Jordan from Koinonia Farm to speak in chapel while he was on one of his Eastern tours. The next day Dr. Enslin, in no uncertain terms, denounced Jordan's chapel lecture calling it "theological tap dancing."

We produced our share of the post-World War baby boom on the campus. Children were a part of campus life. Our oldest daughter Donna was born at Chester Hospital. George and Nancy Lawrence had two children, the Medds had one and the Cheneys had one child. The Davis and Prichard families had children.

Although I still had the GI Bill and we were later moved from the old president's home into nice new brick apartments, I needed to supplement our income because of our growing family. I did a lot of typing for the librarian Mr. Starr. Mr. Starr was compiling a Baptist bibliography, composed of everything written by and about Baptists. My assignment was to type index cards to be filed and used later in the bibliography. It was my pleasure to see the twelve volumes of Starr's work many years later at Colgate Rochester Seminary.

I also worked part-time at Sears in downtown Chester in the paint and hardware departments on Friday and Saturday nights. After work we would frequently go upstairs to the apartment of Jane and Ed Spath, who happened to be one of the very few on the campus who had a television set.

One summer I served as camp director of Camp Sunshine and Clarice was camp nurse. My youngest sister Pauline came up for the summer to keep an eye on and take care of our two children. It was to be a memorable summer for Pauline as well as for Clarice and me. It was a "fresh air" camp. Children from Philadelphia were referred by their teachers and invited to attend the three-week camp. There were three weeks for boys and three weeks for girls.

The big goal of the board of directors was to see that the children were kept clean and well fed. They had some sort of medical checkup on entering the camp. Records were kept to see how much weight the kids put on in their three weeks of camping.

Alec, a fine black man, who was Chief Chef at Swarthmore College was camp cook and he was great. Crab cakes were his specialty and they were the best I have ever eaten. The camp had a pond and the kids got to go swimming every day. I had bought an old car for the summer and had to use it once to carry two homesick disruptive kids home at night. I sold the car when the summer was over.

Pauline did a great job of taking care of our children and I think she had a nice tour of Philadelphia before returning to Georgia. She rode the train alone to Philadelphia. Aunt Luna, who lived in Philadelphia, was to meet Pauline at the train station but was not there when she arrived. She phoned Luna and was informed that Luna's son Charles was on the way to pick her up. Pauline was surprised since Charles was even younger than she was. However, he knew his way around Philadelphia. Pauline remembers seeing Joe Dimaggio at a baseball game and he has been her baseball hero ever since.

Aunt Winnie died while we lived in Chester. Dad came up for the funeral and we went to New York. Aunt Winnie lived on Long Island in Kew Gardens. I had visited them in 1939 when they invited me for the New York World's Fair. This time I was surprised at how drab their apartment looked some ten or twelve years later. Edward Abbott's fortunes must have declined greatly in the years following my visit when we went to the World's Fair.

## Inter-Seminary Conferences

While at Crozer, I attended two inter-seminary conferences, one at Union Seminary in New York City and the other at Princeton.

At Union, a couple of us were fortunate enough to stay in the president's apartment. We had to use two keys to enter at night. I don't remember what we did outside the seminary as we were at Morningside Heights. I remember seeing Dr. Rhinehold Niebuhr, probably the best known member of the Union faculty at that time.

I remember more about the Princeton conference. One memorable event was the aloofness of the general seminary students from New York who were Episcopal. They had their own closed communion service that excluded the rest of us, but they gladly participated in the beer-drinking happy hour sessions.

The most memorable event was meeting Dr. Albert Einstein as he strolled across the Princeton campus late one afternoon. He was dressed in his usual gray sweatshirt and baggy slacks. He seemed to have the largest, friendly brown eyes of any person I have ever met. The Princeton students told us that his residence was very near the seminary and he would occasionally visit the students and bring them cookies his sister had baked. They told us they once asked Dr. Einstein if he could explain his theory of relativity in simple layman's terms, so that a theology student could understand it. His answer was one simple word, "No."

There were also memorable student trips to Valley Forge, China Town in Philadelphia, and a visit to Father Divine's Heaven in West Philadelphia. Clarice and other student wives went with us. The visit to Father Divine's Heaven was "The Event!"

## Father Divine's Heaven

As Father Divine's "communion" service was always held late at night, we had a long wait for his arrival. When we were seated, women were on one side of the room and men on the other. However, students and other guests could not sit next to one another. We were seated first but had to leave a vacant chair between us. When the followers of Father Divine arrived they took the empty seats with us at the communion table. The man across from me had been a member of the Philadelphia symphony orchestra, or so he told me. He was in a wheelchair. He said, "When I look into your eyes, Father Divine is looking through my eyes into your eyes."

When Father Divine arrived, there was a great flurry of activity. His closest followers dressed in special robes hovered near him – all females and, as I believe they were called rosebuds and lilybuds. The lilybuds were "spotless virgins" and the rosebuds were "slightly tainted."

Members turned all of their earnings over to Father Divine and he in turn provided them food, clothing, and shelter. I remember a famous picture from *Life* magazine of Father Divine's followers with several suitcases filled with small bills to be used in the purchase of some kind of building. It took the bank tellers several hours to count the money.

The communion meal remains the most memorable meal of my life. Food was served family style and on fancy plates with nice napkins. All food first came to Father Divine. He had mirrors in front of him, on his right, and on his left so he could see behind and tell which food was coming up. He then knew whether to pick up a silver fork or silver spoon to place on the dish. Thus he touched every plate of food and so "blessed" it. Plates were then passed to his left and to his right.

I decided to watch the members and take what they took. First came the cold cuts: cheese, bologna, ham, salads, and so forth. The members passed them on and so did I. Then came plenty of bread, finally broiled fish, chicken, ham, and steak. Now the members were digging in, and so did I.

All plates were in duplicate, unseasoned and unsalted for the diabetics and then the seasoned and salted food. For desserts there were cakes and pies and finally three huge punch bowls filled with ice cream: vanilla, strawberry, and chocolate. All were artistically decorated with a candy flower on top. In all, it was a 52-course meal, but served in duplicate so there were 104 dishes in all.

During the entire meal some of his rosebuds or lilybuds were kneeling and facing and "adoring" Father Divine. He also had his "spotless virgin" white Canadian wife seated at his side. After the meal and near midnight he departed in his stretched limousine. Several of his followers ran after his car into the dark night. Yes, the visit to "Father Divine's Heaven" was truly a memorable experience for seminary students.

## Martin Luther King, Jr.

The *Atlanta Constitution* noted on December 6, 1999 that a memorial would be built honoring Martin Luther King, Jr. on the mall in Washington, D.C. This was a very fine step for the nation to take.

In reflecting back on my two years with Martin Luther King, Jr. (he was always called M. L. at the seminary, although I believe his close friend Walter McCall sometimes called him Mike), I don't recall that he really stood out in my mind. Walter was also a graduate of Morehouse College and came up to Crozer with M. L. King. M. L. was one of several black students and I knew Walter McCall better than I knew M. L.

However, we had students from several foreign countries that gave us new opportunities to learn and make friends. China, Japan, Egypt and Panama had one student each from those countries. We also had a Quaker from Maine, a radical from Mississippi, a classmate whose wife was from Australia, and students from a number of states in the eastern United States.

I first met M. L. King, Jr. and his father at the beginning of my first year at Crozer. M. L. Senior had driven up from Atlanta to bring his son back for his second year of studies. Although I was several years older than M. L., he was one year ahead of me.

Initially I was much more impressed with the father than with the son. "Daddy" King (as his congregation called him) was a large man. In September of 1949 he was dressed in a dark suit with a heavy gold watch chain across his midsection. He had his large car parked in front of Old Main. My first impression was that he was a bit pompous and overbearing for a Baptist preacher. In looking back, I am sure that I made the judgment out of my cultural background just as "Daddy" King was from his.

During the year, I got to know M. L. much better. He was always pleasant, friendly, serious, and rather "bookish." A scholar in the classic sense, he always seemed to be well prepared in class. However, as he was one year ahead of me, I don't believe I had more than one class with him.

He had an excellent reputation as a student preacher. He had a remarkable, gifted speaking voice. When it was M. L.'s turn to speak in chapel, everybody turned out to hear him. (Chapel was not mandatory at Crozer.) Faculty as well as students were present. Crozer had a pool table in the basement directly under the chapel and no pool balls were heard clicking when M. L. preached.

Once, A. J. Muste, at the invitation of my classmate Walter Stark, spoke on nonviolence. A. J. Muste was Executive Secretary of FOR, Fellowship of Reconciliation. He spoke on the pacifist movement of Mohandas Gandhi. M. L. began a rather heated discussion with Mr. Muste over this. There were about a dozen of us seated near the big piano in one of the formal lounges in Old Main. Muste was quite old and had in past years a rich experience in the cause of pacifism. At any rate, M. L. was quite willing to take him on in debate.

After I became associate pastor of Chester's ancient First Baptist Church, a group of women approached me and asked me to recommend a black student to speak to their organization and asked if I would come with him. I immediately thought of M. L., asked him, and he quickly accepted. The women's group allowed M. L. to choose his own topic and he chose, "Christianity and Capitalism."

The one line I remember from his speech was, "most of us are not capitalists, we are only potential capitalists." Those may not have been his exact words, but that is as I remember them. At any rate, the women seemed to be favorably impressed with his talk.

At the beginning of his senior year, he was elected president of the student body, an honor which in turn was conferred on me the following year.

M. L. writes of having visited in our apartment several times. I am sure that he did and he may have kept Lonnie for us on occasion when we went out for the evening. We did correspond after he left Crozer for graduate school to pursue his doctorate.

Later, I telephoned him at Montgomery, AL, after his home was bombed on January 30th, 1956. He appreciated the call and I have the letter that he wrote to me following that crime.

Crozer Seminary

THE MONTGOMERY IMPROVEMENT ASSOCIATION
1903 Myles Street
Phone 5-3364
Montgomery 8, Alabama

Office of the President            March 19, 1956

Dear Friends:

This is just a note to express my deepest gratitude to you for your kind letter. Such letters from friends sympathetic with our momentous struggle for justice give us renewed vigor and courage to carry on.

With every good wish, I am

                         Cordially yours,

                         M. L. King, Jr.,
                         President.

MLK/ehr

1956 Letter to Francis from Martin Luther King, Jr.

A few years later, I traveled from Monticello to Nashville during Christmas for a meeting sponsored by the Fellowship of Southern Churchmen. M. L. spoke to the group on that occasion. It was just after Charlene Hunter and Hamilton Holmes had enrolled at the University of Georgia in Athens. Charlene was in attendance at that meeting.

Dr. Sam Williams, a black minister and teacher from Atlanta, made the classic statement for me. In polling the current state of love and brotherhood among Southern churches, Dr. Sam stated, "... among Baptists in Atlanta, Dr. Louie D. Newton calls the tune. Dear Dr. Newton. Dr. Newton can smell a can of beer all the way across Atlanta, but he cannot find it in his heart or in the word of God to say one word against the evils of segregation."

I also remember going to Atlanta for a meeting when Martin Luther King, Jr. first moved back to Atlanta from Montgomery to head the Southern Christian Leadership Conference (SCLC) work and to be associate pastor with his father. This had been the longtime dream of Martin Luther King, Senior. I do not remember who sponsored the meeting, probably the Georgia Council of Human Relations or the Council of Southern Churches.

The meeting was held at the old Luckie Street YMCA building. This was about the only place in Atlanta at that time that was integrated and would also serve meals. A false alarm brought dozens of police cars and fire trucks roaring up to the building. A photographer assigned to the governor's office was going around taking photos of those in attendance. He always got real excited and took a bunch of photos whenever he could catch a black man and a white woman seated together and talking to each other.

The night service was held at the old First Congregational Church in downtown Atlanta. There was a fair-sized crowd. I met Coretta Scott King there for the first and only time.

Finally, the last time I saw M. L. and heard him speak was when we were living in Statesville, NC, and he was speaking at the Johnson C. Smith University in Charlotte. This was only a year or less before he was killed in Memphis.

The place was ringed with policemen and there was no way I could get close enough to speak to him. By that time there had been numerous threats against his life. He had been questioned repeatedly about his nonviolent approach to dealing with segregation and whether he still believed in it after Selma, Birmingham, and all the bombings and shootings of those practicing nonviolence.

## Crozer Seminary

He alluded to the possibility that he might not live much longer, but that it didn't matter. He had been to the mountaintop and seen the promised land. I think he used some of the same words he had used in his famous Christmas sermon broadcast over the Canadian Broadcasting System. The words I remember are:

> "They keep asking me, if I still believe in nonviolence. I want to assure you that even if some day I am the last man on earth who believes in nonviolence, I will still believe in nonviolence and will believe in it with every fiber of my being!"

A final note before the account of his funeral. We had moved back to Atlanta from North Carolina and I was working in the state Economic Opportunity Office in downtown Atlanta. For some reason I decided to attend the Monday morning meeting of the Baptist preachers. Usually they met at the Georgia Baptist Hospital on Boulevard Avenue. However, a decision had been made for the white and black Baptist ministers to meet together. It so happened that for years the two groups had been meeting on Boulevard Street on Monday mornings and only about two blocks apart, but never meeting together until this occasion.

Dr. M. L. King, Sr. recounted the numerous, anonymous threats against the life of his son and how calls would come to him at night and saying to him, "This is so-and-so funeral home, we have your son's body. What do you want us to do with it?" He said these calls were always from white people and the black ministers were in great distress over the lack of brotherhood and the silence of the white pulpits. Note: This was several years after I had left Monticello and after I had been fired from Hopewell Baptist Church for speaking out on our double standard of justice in our communities and in the South.

I was in Macon talking to a widowed schoolteacher about some of her problems with trying to teach and maintain some sort of discipline in a predominately black school. It had been a terrific cultural shock to her.

How much greater was the shock a few minutes later when we learned that Martin Luther King, Jr. had been shot while attending a meeting in Memphis, TN. Atlanta the next day was also in a state of shock, as was the nation. Riots and looting broke out in Washington, D.C. and many other great cities in the nation. This was not so in Atlanta.

Later I joined the long line of visitors paying final respects to Martin Luther King, Jr. at the Sisters Chapel, Spelman College. I believe that I was in line for more than six hours as the double column line snaked and wound around and doubled back all across the campus and out into the streets.

Martin Luther King, Jr. was in what looked like a mahogany casket. We moved quickly by as thousands of others were following. Coming out of the chapel, I remember being stared at by an extremely stern-faced white man in some kind of uniform. My guess is that he was some kind of FBI agent who acted under some assumption that the killer would return to see his victim and that the FBI agent would be able to detect some note of satisfaction or jubilation over such a dastardly deed. At any rate, I stared back at him just as hard, because I was curious about that man and what must have been going through his mind. I also wondered then, and still wonder, exactly why he was there and who sent him.

Atlanta streets were deserted on the day of the funeral, at least in the early morning hours when I went in to work. State employees were not given a holiday and I learned on arrival at the office that Lester Maddox had called out the National Guard. However, my boss, Mr. E. C. Bryant, said, "This town is dead." Nothing was going on. Later Lou Thomas and Cynthia Perkins from our office and I walked down to Hurt Park at Georgia State University, across the street from the old Municipal Auditorium.

Crowds were beginning to assemble along the street and many were listening on their portable radios to the funeral services at Ebenezer Baptist Church. The press of crowds around the old church was very great. A few good singers and a very large black woman with an extremely powerful voice led the way of the singers. They locked arms and began marching 20 abreast from curb to curb and began drawing off hundreds of people as they marched away toward Morehouse College across to the west side of the city. This was probably a wise move as I learned that the crowd was jammed building to building and street to street up and down Auburn Ave.

Finally the old wagon, drawn by a team of tired mules came carrying the coffin and escorted by members of the SCLC and all wearing bib overalls. How symbolic of all of the hundreds and thousands of black men who toiled throughout their lives behind a team of mules as they sought to scratch out a living as tenants on southern cotton farms or worked plowing gardens for white people and planting small truck gardens on the side.

Following the SCLC honor guard with their black arm bands who watched the old wagon and tried to keep the coffin from bouncing around too much, there came the honor escorts and famous folks: Wilt "the Stilt" Chamberlain towering over everyone else, Harry Belafonte, Sammy Davis Jr., Eartha Kitt, Nelson and Happy Rockefeller, the Metropolitan of the

Greek Orthodox Church of New York City, Senator Jacob Javitts, Bobby Kennedy, New York's Mayor Lindsey, and many, many others. This group had all locked arms, presenting something of a solid street-to-street, curb-to-curb New York line.

The young blacks would swarm around Bobby Kennedy every time the throng had to stop. Soon Lindsey and Rockefeller were dropping back and away from Kennedy. Lou Thomas, Cynthia Perkins and I stepped off the curb and into the march after we had been watching for some minutes. To this day, I do not know how we ended up directly behind Eartha Kitt, the Rockefellers, and Bobby Kennedy.

As we passed the state capitol we noticed that it was literally ringed with National Guardsmen. The crowd looked, but paid little attention. I am sure the capitol building flag was at full staff, although a half block away the City Hall flag was at half staff. I remember one black lady speaking as we passed the state capitol, "Don't you worry, Mr. Maddox, we're not thinking about you today."

As we walked up the hill on Hunter Street and across the Techwood viaduct, I could look back and see a solid river of humanity in the line of march. It was truly an awesome sight.

I learned later that Nelson Rockefeller had been up most of the night at the Regency Hotel as he talked long distance with members of the New York State General Assembly. As a result, New York passed some of the most far-reaching urban and social development legislation ever passed to that time.

I wonder how history would have changed if Richard Nixon had also chosen to join the march. I understand than he did attend the services at Ebenezer. The campus green at Dr. King's beloved Morehouse College was covered and Dr. Mays delivered an eloquent message. "They killed the dreamer, but they cannot kill the dream."

## Martin Luther King, Jr.'s Letters to Francis Stewart

The originals of three letters from Martin Luther King, Jr. to me were donated to Colgate Rochester Crozer Divinity School in Rochester, New York. Colgate Rochester Crozer is the successor to Crozer Seminary.

Crozer Seminary

The following letter was hand written and some of the words have become illegible. My transcript of the letter follows:

27 Colden St.<br>
Roxbury, Massachusetts<br>
July 26, 1954

Dear Francis,

It was certainly a happy experience to hear your voice the other day after such a long time. I had a very fine trip back to Boston, and fortunately I stopped by in Chester and got some idea of what is taking place at Crozer. I found all the things you told me quite authentic. It is definitely true that Enslin, Prichard and Batton are leaving. Prichard is going to some school in California. Enslin was retired, and Batton has gone into the Episcopal church.

I have not been able to get the exact causal factor that led to the great turnover in faculty but think that at bottom it was out of conflict with Blanton. I think that he had been desirous of getting rid of them from the very beginning. Now the whole faculty will consist of men that he hired directly.

What the outcome will be I don't know. I hope that it won't be disastrous. I understand that a man from Eastern will replace Enslin.

As for me, I am doing fine and working hard to complete this (illegible).

Brother, it really requires a lot of work. I said to you the other night that I have been called to a church in Montgomery, Alabama. My wife and I will be moving in around the first of September. It is a very fine church with even greater possibilities. I hope that we will do a good job there. When we get settled in and get the program going, I will want to have you over to preach for us.

Please give my best regards to you lovely wife and to the kids. I look forward to seeing them in the near future. I hope for your continued success in your pastorate. When you have time, be sure to write me a line.

Sincerely Yours,
Martin King

## Crozer Seminary

The following letter was written by Dr. King while recovering from a nearly-fatal stab wound he received while signing his books in Harlem.

**Martin Luther King, Jr.**
Dexter Ave. Baptist Church
454 Dexter Avenue
Montgomery, Ala.
Amherst 3-3970

October 23, 1958.

Dear Francis:

Thank you for your kind letter of October 2nd. I enjoyed reading it so much.

Your thoughtful gesture will remain dear to me as long as the cords of memory shall lengthen. They come as a source of great spiritual strength and are of inestimable value in giving me the courage to face the ordeal of this trying period.

I am happy to hear that you enjoyed reading my book and hope that it may be some measure of help in these turbulent times.

I am happy to report that I am well on the road to a complete recovery. I solicit your prayers and continued good wishes as I prepare to rejoin the ranks of those who are working tirelessly and ceaselessly for the realization of the ideals of Freedom, Brotherhood and Human Dignity.

Sincerely yours,

Martin Luther King, Jr.

MLK:p

The Reverend Francis E. Stewart
Monticello Baptist Church
Monticello, Georgia

P.S. I hope our paths will cross in the not to distant future

1958 Letter to Francis from Martin Luther King, Jr.

# Monticello

## 1952 - 1964

Following Crozer Seminary we moved to Monticello, Georgia, where I was called to pastor the Monticello Baptist Church. I also served as pastor of Hopewell Baptist Church in Jasper County on every fourth Sunday for several years while in Monticello.

Other than serving as assistant pastor at Tattnall Square Baptist Church in Macon and assistant pastor of the First Baptist Church in Chester, Pennsylvania, my only other pastorate was Gibbs Memorial Baptist at Bostwick, GA, while I was a Mercer student, and Powelton Baptist Church in Hancock County the year I was a chaplain intern at Milledgeville State Hospital.

Francis in Monticello Baptist Church

Monticello is the county seat of Jasper County in middle Georgia. In 1952 it was a somewhat isolated, old cotton-farming community that lost out during the boll weevil epidemic in the early 1920s. The cotton warehouse had fallen into decay and the old roof had fallen in. Several farmers had tried growing peaches and this was fairly successful. However, refrigeration was a problem and the freight rates were against shipping from south to north. Plus, peaches needed plenty of refrigeration and were often spoiled by the time they reached northern markets.

Growing pine trees seemed to be the largest farming enterprise by the early 1950s. A few dairy farms, a few poultry farms and a few beef farms, but mostly pine trees covered Jasper County. This is still true in 1999. Plus, there is a large portion of federal government-owned timber in the Piedmont Wildlife Refuge and the Oconee National Forrest.

The entire county in the 1950s was only slightly over 8,000 in population. There were a number of churches in the county serving both the white and black populations. Methodist, Baptist, and Presbyterians, but no Catholic churches, and in this part of Georgia, no Jewish synagogues.

Monticello Baptist Church had a membership of perhaps 300, although a significant portion had moved away or were inactive. However, the town and the church were quite old with a history dating back to the early 1800s. The town was not burned when Sherman marched his army through in the fall of 1864.

The Methodist, Baptist, and Presbyterian churches held union worship services on Sunday nights during the summer months. Not many folks wanted to go to church on hot summer nights, plus most of these folks were related in one way or another. It was often said, "Three churches, but one congregation."

The town had a lot of widows, close to 100, and very few widowers. Some were very elderly and quite frail. Others were active and enjoyed meeting and playing bridge, etc. Among the men, the gathering places were the drugstore, the restaurant, and the courthouse. Topics of conversation revolved around the weather, hunting, fishing, football and, around election time, politics. I do not know what the women talked about when they had their meetings.

Monticello, was a rather isolated town and community. Forty or more miles to Macon, 15 or 16 miles east to Eatonton; about the same distance west to Jackson and some 25-30 miles southeast to Milledgeville. There were no paved roads into the county until around 1928. In earlier years, teams had to ford the Ocmulgee River on the west side of the county.

## Monticello

Naturally, teams could not cross when the river was high although a ferry was built for crossing in the area.

My strength as a pastor was visiting the sick at the new local Hill-Burton hospital, visiting the sick and shut-ins in the community (not restricted to visiting only the Baptists), and visiting the sick when they were hospitalized in Macon or Atlanta. I visited those who did not belong to or attend any church. I also visited the local county jail. This was not appreciated by some wardens who said prisoners were there for punishment only. Other prison guards seemed to appreciate my visits.

There were no nursing homes in the vicinity. However, there was a nursing home in Jones County to the south. A former schoolhouse had been converted into a nursing home. Not a very neat or attractive facility, but established by a man who saw a need and tried to meet it.

One of the recurring pleas from the elderly women was for the establishment of nursing homes for those no longer able to care for themselves. This led to my proposing to the Georgia Baptist Convention at its annual meeting to make a study of the need and report back in one year. The study led to the establishment of the first Georgia Baptist Retirement Home in the Baptist Village at Waycross, GA.

Monticello was a wonderful place for our children. Both Susan and Kathy were born in Monticello. Frank and Donna were small children in 1952, when we first moved there. Although our home, the Baptist pastorium, was very close to the street, there was not a lot of traffic and the home was only one block from the town square. If the children wandered off, they were known by everyone in town and thus not likely to get lost. In addition, the home was next to the football flat, a great place for the children to play whenever it was not in use by football players.

Because we lived in Monticello for twelve years, it was the only home the children knew and one that they would remember long after we moved away. In fact it was hard on the children when we told them we were moving. It was only later that they acknowledged they were glad we had left Monticello to learn about a bigger world.

Clarice had a ready job as a nurse in the Monticello hospital, usually working in the operating room when surgery was scheduled and, on occasion, doing private duty nursing. That, plus the home, kept her very busy.

I was constantly bombarded by the state Baptist officials to "promote the program." Those were not the exact words they always used, but that is what it amounted to: Sunday school conventions, Training Union "M" nights, state conventions, association meetings, singing conventions, student night at Christmas, fund-raising events for state, home and foreign missions, invitations to teach a class during January Bible study week and on and on.

But there was plenty of activity in the town. I felt that a minister in a small town should minister to and witness to the total life of the total community. That led me to become active in the local Kiwanis Club serving on committees and, for one year, as president of the local club. Later I served as chairperson of the Better Hometown contest, a program sponsored by the Georgia Power Company. During my year as chairperson, we received the top award, "Champion of Champion Hometowns". We received a cash award to the town plus a nice banquet and newspaper publicity.

Better Home Town Contest planning group, left to right: Ben Warren, Helen Dickinson, Francis Stewart, Nellie Pritchett.

1954 Better Home Town Sweepstakes award, left to right: Audrey Ezell, Georgia Power Representative Harley Branch, Clarice Stewart, Francis Stewart, and Mayor Ray Persons.

Jasper County received a grant from the Farmer's Home Administration to build a water tower, which enabled the Georgia Pacific plant to be built in Monticello. Grant proposal team, left to right: William Kicks Key, Dr. Smith (dentist), Mayor Ray Persons, Laree Benton, Francis Stewart.

My preaching eventually got me in a lot of hot water. I had been placed on the "watch" list in my early years at Monticello when Chuck Evans (pastor of a nearby Baptist Church and later Baptist missionary to Africa) and I made a motion at the annual Central Baptist Association meeting to "...recognize the Supreme Court's ruling on school segregation as the supreme law of the land." This was in the early 1950s and shortly after the Supreme Court ruling declaring "separate but equal" as unconstitutional.

One of us made the motion and the other seconded the motion. That should have brought it to the floor for discussion, but one old Doctor immediately called, "Table the motion." And it was tabled. Later the good doctor said he wanted it, not only tabled but, "thrown under the table."

The state had predicted the Supreme Court might make such a ruling and Governor Herman Talmadge managed to get a 3-percent sales tax passed to begin constructing separate-but-equal school buildings. (I do not recall that anything was said in the law about the quality or qualifications of the teachers.) It did result in a flurry of construction of red brick buildings across the state. However in 15 or 20 years, most of these buildings were either integrated or turned into some kind of community building, such as alcohol treatment, mental health, or mental retardation workshops.

Still later, when I preached at Hopewell Baptist Church from the book of Amos, "Let justice roll down like waters," and pointed out our double standard of justice in the county, such as no blacks on our juries, it brought down a rain of fire on me and our household. I was dismissed from the rural, every fourth Sunday, Hopewell Baptist Church. Some of the men would turn their backs on me when they met me on the street. Our children began to wonder why they were not being invited to some of the children's activities, as they had been in the past.

We had a wonderful black physician named Dr. Funderburg who served both white and black folks. His office was in fact the only truly integrated spot in the whole county. At one time he invited George McMaster and me to accompany him to a meeting in Atlanta. We accepted, but it seems most of the people in town knew about it almost before we left the town limits. "What in the world do those preachers think they are doing?" "Where are they going?" "What are they up to now?" We were surely the talk of the town that day. And we heard plenty about it when we got back to Monticello.

At one point, George McMaster and I each picked a member from our churches – a Presbyterian elder and a Baptist deacon – to meet with us in Dr. Funderburg's office. I don't remember what we discussed, but I do remember what the deacon said to me after the meeting.

"Preacher, that was hard for me to take. I don't believe I am as prejudiced as my parents were, and I hope things will be better, but that was HARD for me to take." And after my dismissal from Hopewell Baptist Church, one of the women, the only one who did not vote in the called meeting to dismiss me said, "I have been going to church all my life, but this is the first time I have ever heard a preacher say that we were not treating Negroes right." So in her mind, I was preaching against all of the other preachers she had heard in her entire life.

The local dentist, Dr. Smith, was my fishing buddy. He was a dedicated fisherman – summer, fall, winter, spring. In wintertime he would build a small fire and then put it out and stand in the warm soil and ashes to keep his feet warm. The fall, during hunting season, was perhaps his and my favorite time to fish. Few fishermen were about as most sportsmen were trying to get their trophy buck. We fished in local farm ponds and occasionally we would go over to Rock Eagle State Park. Dr. Smith once told me that a former preacher that he took fishing kept talking about how beautiful and peaceful the woods and sky looked. Dr. Smith was a serious fisherman and did not appreciate talk about anything but fishing when he took someone with him. He said, "I did not invite him again."

Dr. Smith was also the one who spoke up for me when others were trying to run me out of town. In the men's Sunday School class he said, "Now we may not agree with our pastor, but he has a right to say what he believes God has called him to preach. And furthermore, we do not need a bunch of outsiders to come in and tell us how to run our church." That was what kept me from being fired at Monticello Baptist Church, as I had been at Hopewell Church.

The mentality of some older, rural white males of the old plantation cotton and post-Civil War period baffled me. In the early 1950s Jasper County was sort of a backwater place. This was just prior to the full impact of the Civil Rights movement and the powerful drama revealed in the nightly television news.

Years later I wrote the following account of the early Monticello period in my journal. (Volume VI, page 85 ff):

> The Little Nigger Boy Theory
>
> In many ways this is the oldest and most deeply ingrained theory. The older and more affluent southerners (in these parts anyway) practiced this and by and large it proved most effective as it probably dated back to slavery houseboy training days.
>
> Whenever an elderly affluent (always affluent) small town southerner, be they man or woman starts out to do a task, be it cleaning out the cellar, cutting weeds, mowing the lawn or fishing, the first prerequisite is a "little nigger boy."
>
> Boys seemed to have more appeal than girls. Why? I am not exactly certain. I suppose there was always a dream that he might develop into that now exceedingly rare, loyal,

devoted multipurpose "Old Tom" Negro who will work in the yard, sweep, cook, scrub floors, or even patch socks and with a high degree of skill and also complete dedication.

At any rate "little nigger boys" were around in abundance hanging from the back of a pickup truck on the way to "the farm" or riding in the open trunk of a car while holding on to a power mower, a sort of boy tow rope.

The "little nigger boy" also provided both amusement and companionship of sorts. He is full of energy and will ask questions. His questions reveal both his ignorance, his desire to learn, and extreme naivete.

I well remember an incident when I discovered a lot of lime spilled along the railroad tracks at a farmers supply warehouse. I asked the manager if I could shovel some for my garden. His reply was. "Certainly! Get you a little nigger boy and take all you want." It was indeed a cultural shock to learn how these southern pseudo-aristocrats were so dependent on "little nigger boys" for the simplest tasks. I was raised on a farm and was used to these simple tasks from the age of seven or eight years and thought nothing of getting my hands dirty on any kind of manual work.

The "Uncle Toms" and females raised in white folks' homes from early childhood were like family, but always as servant Cinderellas.

Those were sentiments I encountered when we moved to Jasper County in the early 1950s.

# Monticello

So many memories of Monticello. It was a wonderful place for small children to grow up. A place where there was always something to talk about, namely one's neighbors. So many colorful characters. I first stayed in the home of Mrs. Monroe Phillips as the pastorium was still in the process of being renovated. Also, a young Dr. Marvin Green was staying there at the same time.

Mrs. Phillips was sort of a matriarch of the community. Even the mayor jumped when she called. A strong-willed, intelligent, fine Christian woman. A direct descendent of Jesse Mercer, the founder of Mercer University.

So many men seemed to thrive on permanent unemployment. Perhaps they were all elderly and lived off social security or their wives. One man spent much of his time in his cabin out by his fish pond. His wife worked in the local hospital. Another, Uncle Willie F. J. of whom it was said, "Never did a day's work in his life," always walked and was trailed by his pack of dogs whenever he came to town. He would buy them an ice cream cone in the local drug store and then dump it on the floor so the dogs could lick it up.

He would also bring nice arrangements of flowers to any woman who took his fancy at the moment. He once brought Clarice a beautiful arrangement of camellias that pleased her very much until she learned that he had picked them from a neighbor's prize bush, as was his custom.

On another occasion when he was younger, he rode his horse up the steps and into the county courthouse. There are several episodes that I remember about Uncle Willie. One was a community Thanksgiving service at the Presbyterian church. Mrs. Owen was the new Methodist minister's wife who always made it a point to be on time and to see that everything was in place. She was early and it was an early morning service. She thought the building was too cold and looking around found Uncle Willie sound asleep on the front pew. Not knowing who he was and assuming that he must be the janitor she proceeded to shake him and awaken him and suggest that the building needed more heat. Uncle Willie shook her off and proceeded to go back to sleep. With that Mrs. Owen demanded, "Aren't you the janitor?" to which Uncle Willie is said to have replied, "Janitor! Hell, I'm an elder in this church." And he proceeded to lie back down. Mrs. Owen was defeated and retreated.

At a wedding ceremony, Uncle Willie, as usual, was about half asleep. But he noticed flashes of light behind him and coming from camera flash bulbs. With each flash he muttered, "Lightning in here."

Once very early on a Sunday morning, I was dressed in slacks and a t-shirt sweeping away leaves in front of the church building steps and sidewalk when Uncle Willie came along all dressed up in his Sunday finest and on his way to church. It was at least three hours before any type of church service. He pulled out a letter from his nephew and suggested that I read it. Then he noticed my garb and said, "You ought to be ashamed of yourself for being dressed like that on the Lord's day," and proceeded to put the letter back in his pocket and march on off to church.

He once said, "If it's in the Bible, I believe it. I believe the whale swallowed Jonah and if the Bible said Jonah swallowed the whale, I would still believe it."

Because we lived next to and overlooking the football field, I was in a perfect position to keep an eye on it all year. I noticed that the grass was not being fertilized as it should, so I slipped down late one evening near dark and proceeded to sprinkle ammonium nitrate in the center of the field, making a big "O" and a cross. Naturally the O and the cross came up dark green, while all around the grass was a dull, pale green. That got the attention of most folks in town and soon after that, improvements were made to the field.

Back before the Civil War, slaves were buried on the church grounds, but not in the same area as the whites. The site where the slave graves were located was north of the pastorium and next to the ball flat. There were no markers and the area was a big weed patch. I decided it would be a good place for a garden, had it plowed and proceeded to have a nice garden there for several years. I now regret that I did not exercise better and more mature judgment. Now I would suggest that the slave cemetery be preserved or at least some sort of marker placed there. It is now the site of the present church building as the old church building and the old pastorium were torn down.

## Clarice

In addition to Clarice's regular work as a surgical nurse at the Monticello Hospital, Clarice sometimes worked as a private duty nurse.

Once Mr. Oscar Holland was in critical condition and possibly would die at any moment. I do not know the nature of his illness, but he was very ill. It was late at night and Mr. Holland was very restless and seemed in great pain. As his nurse, Clarice had done as much as she could to make him comfortable, but he was still very, very uncomfortable.

Finally Clarice asked him if he would like for her to read to him from the Bible. He said, "Yes." Clarice opened the Bible to the 23rd Psalm. As she started reading, Mr. Holland started quoting it along with her. He seemed in great pain, as if every word was a battle to make the words come out. He persisted to the end of the short Psalm and then seemed to become quiet and extremely calm, as if he were dead. Clarice thought that he may be dying.

During this time she seemed aware of a very powerful, mystical presence, as if the room were full of some kind of powerful light. It was some kind of transcendental experience. Mr. Holland had fallen into a deep sleep.

The next morning the doctor was amazed at the vast improvement in Mr. Holland's condition. He lived for another five or more years and appeared to be in good health.

The strangest part of this episode is that later as Clarice talked with Mr. Holland, he too remembered the strange mysterious time exactly as Clarice remembered. It was something that had happened to both of them that night. They were caught up in something powerful, overwhelming, and mystical. Some might call it the Holy Spirit, others might call it something else. However, it is something that once experienced is forever etched deep in one's memory.

Perhaps the two of them were spiritually aware persons. If Mr. Holland had been a different person, or if Clarice had not been the deeply empathic person that she is, the event might not have occurred.

## The LORD Is My Shepherd

A Psalm of David

1   The LORD is my shepherd; I shall not want.

2   He maketh me to lie down in green pastures:

He leadeth me beside the still waters.

3   He restoreth my soul:

He leadeth me in the paths of righteousness for His name's sake.

4   Yea, though I walk through the valley of the shadow of death,

I will fear no evil: for Thou art with me;

Thy rod and thy staff they comfort me.

5   Thou preparest a table before me in the presence of mine enemies:

Thou anointest my head with oil; my cup runneth over.

6   Surely goodness and mercy shall follow me all the days of my life:

and I will dwell in the house of the LORD for ever.

Psalms 23

## Our Young Family

Our young family loved the small town and rural life in and around Monticello. The kids had the run of town and often played in the woods, where they felt perfectly safe. Everyone looked out for everyone else's children in town.

The children especially enjoyed Christmas time when we would be invited to a nearby farm to hunt for that perfect cedar tree. On the Fourth of July, we would get up bright and early before the day got hot and go out into the county to pick blackberries along the side of a dirt road. The kids would soon tire of the thorns and play hide-n-seek in an adjoining corn field. Usually we did manage to get enough blackberries for pie.

(Front row) Kathy, Susan, (middle row) Donna, Lonnie, (back row) Clarice, Francis

## Our Kids Tell All – (Notes from Journal, 1952 - 1963)

### 1952, Lonnie (now called Frank) at Crozer

One evening at Crozer, Lonnie came in with a report to his mother, "You know this little Gospel light of mine?"

"Yes, what about it?" Clarice replied.

"Well, I was playing down by the bank and it rolled down the bank and fell in the creek and I lost it."

### August 1953, Donna reports to her mother

"I want to climb the roof like Joseph Gasses."

Mother: "You might fall off."

Donna: "Well, I can be a pecan."

Mother: "Yes, and you would be a nut, too."

### September 1953, Donna's pet worm

"I am going upstairs to see Mrs. Spot." (her worm)

Clarice: "Where is she?"

Donna: "She's in the clothes hamper."

Clarice goes up to check on Donna.

Clarice: "Donna, what are you doing – eating a worm?"

Donna: "No, I'm just kissing it."

### September 1953, Susan Arrives!

Susan makes her first appearance. Born 4:37 AM, 8 pounds, 1.75 ounces.

Born with her fingers in her mouth (almost). Born in less than 15 minutes. Good lungs!

### August 30, 1954, Lonnie Begins School

After three weeks of saying he is not going to school:

"I don't want to go to school, but I want to know what they do over there, so I guess I will go anyway."

### Lonnie in Indian Garb

"I am Deer Horn One Feather."

### Donna talking about Lonnie

"I call him Son Thomas."

And, talking about Billy Key, "I call him Black Pete."

### January 28, 1956, We welcome Kathy!

Grace Kathryn is born at Monticello hospital. Much excitement for Lonnie, Donna and Susan.

### March 1956, Susan gets the dog in trouble

Clarice: "Susan, how did you get so dirty?"

Susan: "Lonnie did it."

Clarice: "Lonnie is in school."

Susan: "Donna did it."

Clarice: "Donna is in school."

Susan: "Doggie did it. I tell him mother and him mother pank him bottom."

### May 1956, While at Dr. Smith's Garden

The McMaster, Stewart, and Fannin families (Presbyterian, Baptist, and Methodist ministers) shared a part of Dr. Smith's garden.

Susan walking up the hill from the garden: "Carry me Daddy. I'm too heavy to walk."

### Susan and the Giant

Susan at the foot of the stairs, lying rigid and stretched out

Susan: "Mother! Mother, come and help me!"

Clarice: "What's the matter?"

Susan: "A giant has me."

## March 1957, Jackson Lake Picnic with Fannins

We go out to Jackson Lake and have a hot dog picnic with the Fannins.

Little Burch Jr. slips on a rock and falls in the lake and plunges under the water. I was standing beside him and immediately pulled him out. Now the Methodists are saying that I pushed him in and secretly baptized him.

I say, "Not so. Naturally, I had to pull him out because the Methodists have an aversion to deep water."

But the Presbyterians, as usual, have the last word. They say, "It was all predestined."

## Playing Indians

Susan after playing with Timmy Carnes:

"Timmy is going to grow up and be a big Indian and carry a knife. I'm going to grow up and carry a fork."

## December 21, 1957

Our tenth wedding anniversary.

## Kathy's Prayer

Dear God, Thank you for the lady who gave me the doll (Mrs. Berta Giddens) and thank you for Mrs. Ashurst and Miss Eula and thank you for Momma, Daddy and Lonnie, Donna, and Susan and thank you for myself. Amen

## April 1960, Watching TV

"Kathy, who were the ladies we saw on TV last night?"

Kathy: "Oh I remember, they were Isn'ts." (Correct answer: Nuns)

## September 1961, A Cold Leg

Kathy in Benton Supply Store:

Clerk: "Kathy, aren't you cold today with those shorts and short sleeves on?"

Kathy: "No. The only spot on me that was cold was on my leg and I put a Bandaid over it."

## 1961, Lonnie writes on my calendar

June 7$^{th}$, 14$^{th}$, 21$^{st}$, and 28$^{th}$: Baseball game

## Monday, August 20$^{th}$, 1962

Lonnie starts football camp (age 14).

## April 1963, Friday night Rough House

Friday was stay-up-late night and, occasionally, "Rough House" night with popcorn. The kids got to wrestle dad until someone started crying.

Kathy, after having her picture taken sound asleep: "I decided I would go ahead and go to sleep."

## August 1963

Lonnie starts football camp.

## October 1963, Lonnie's birthday

Lonnie begins piano lessons.

## Kathy

In January of 1964, a great tragedy in our lives also was a time for an outpouring of support from the wonderful people of Monticello and Jasper County.

At the age of seven, our youngest daughter Kathy came down with measles, which developed into encephalitis. Kathy was rushed to the hospital on January first and she died on January third. This beautiful, young light was taken from us.

As we grieved our loss, the entire community came to our comfort.

Grace Kathryn Stewart

# Milledgeville

## 1964-1965

At the time of Kathy's death in January 1964, I had been seeking a call to another church for four years. I no longer felt that we could support our growing family on the salary of $400 a month. I had cashed in my Southern Baptist Retirement fund to pay bills.

I had gone to Big Stone Gap, Virginia, and Sparta, North Carolina, to preach trial sermons. Big Stone Gap was a coal mining town. In winter it was a terribly dreary, drab and depressing place. It was as if even God had abandoned the boarded up town.

Pulpit committees had visited Monticello once or twice but no calls. So I was pleased when the Chaplain program came available at Central State Hospital in Milledgeville, only about 30 miles from Monticello. I had always believed that my pastoral role was much stronger than my preaching and the hospital was a healing time for me, so soon following Kathy's death.

This was not to be the case with the rest of the family. Clarice, many years later, said she regretted that she kept so much grief and hurt bottled up for so many years.

Milledgeville was the state capital during the Civil War and was the site of the very first mental hospital in the state. Part of the old original wall is still standing. We were told that the purpose of the wall was not to keep patients in but to keep outsiders away from the hospital. Georgia State College for Women (now renamed); the state women's prison; state Youth Development Center; state prison for the mentally insane; Colony Farm for aged state prisoners; and the Georgia War Veterans Nursing Home were some of the many state institutions located at Milledgeville.

Because Milledgeville is very near the geographic center of the state, it was a logical location for the old state capital and for the state institutions. However, in later years and during the years of depression, these institutions suffered along with the rest of the state. Because there were so many poor people, and because there were few county homes for the aged, a number of people pressured their doctors and public officials to have family members committed to the mental hospital. Thus, during the 1950s and early 1960s, the population of the state hospital had grown to over 12,000 patients, a population larger than the city of Milledgeville.

Word of patient neglect and abuse began to leak out and Jack Nelson was the reporter assigned by the Atlanta newspapers to begin an investigation. His series of newspaper articles was like a bombshell dropped on the state. It was a real snake-pit story, an account of gross abuse and neglect. Moreover, it was reported that a nurse was actually doing major surgery, hip pin surgery, for the many poor souls who had fallen and broken a leg or hip. The nurse was doing surgery and the surgeon was assisting!

Another account reported finding written on a hospital wall, "They is no God." The long series of articles managed to arouse the voters of the state who demanded that something be done. The two leading lights in the Georgia churches, Bishop Arthur Moore of the Methodist Church, and Dr. Louie D. Newton, former editor of the Baptist paper *The Christian Index* and pastor of Druid Hills Baptist Church, but more popularly known as Georgia's "Baptist Bishop" began to call for money to build chapels at the Hospital. Funds were raised and the Chapels of all Faiths were constructed. Five chapels were constructed.

Moreover, the Georgia General Assembly began to pour money into the complex. New homes were built to house the professional staff. A new staff dormitory, a large central kitchen and bakery, and other additions were made. Also, a concerted effort was made to turn the hospital into a training facility for professional staff: psychiatrists, psychologists, social workers, psychiatric nurses, and chaplains. A leading hospital administrator was recruited and staff salaries were raised. The Georgia Baptists put up money for stipends for chaplain trainees and the state also paid chaplains as well as all other staff.

These were some of the events that led up to my entering the chaplain trainee program in January of 1964. My first session was for three months. I stayed in the dormitory during the week and returned to Monticello only on weekends. Thus, I was largely removed from my family during a time of so much grief.

I was plunged into visits on the wards and encountered so many people with very serious emotional and physical problems. There was very little time to deal with my own grief and loss. For the first time, I met people with Huntington's disease, a disease with no cure, always fatal, but not a mental disease. This disease is hereditary and the patients always know, approximately, when their lives will end.

Two patients I remember, after all these years. One was a patient in the Georgia War Veterans Nursing Home, who said he began to notice a slight tremor while shaving in the morning and gradually he began to cut himself more often as he shaved. The other was a young woman who walked with a slight limp. In both cases, they had been shipped off to Milledgeville, probably because no one in their home, family, or community could care for them. So, far from home, they were cast into the pool of the living dead.

As for me, I could walk off the ward at any time, so I was with them and yet apart.

Another was a beautiful young woman who had several times attempted suicide by cutting her wrists. She offered to show me where she had slashed her buttocks and genitals. I declined to be shown. My supervisor later said I exercised good judgment in setting limits. I learned later that this beautiful young woman had committed suicide at home by taking poison.

Equally startling, was to find people that I had known from prior years. Two were from Monticello. One was a World War II veteran and the other was a former high school football player. The football player said he heard voices. Was it from a football injury? His big disappointment was that his former football coach never came to see him.

The third was a fine young woman who I had dated while we were Mercer students. A mother of three children, her husband, a doctor, had put her away. I don't know how long she remained there, but I hope not long. So many patients never had visits from family or friends. However, there was one big exception.

Each week Jews from the various synagogues in North Georgia would come to Milledgeville. A rabbi would come with them and conduct a Jewish worship service at the Chapel of All Faiths. This service was open to all Jewish patients who could walk to the Chapel. After the worship service, the patients and visitors would all sit down to a meal the visitors had brought with them. These patients had something to look forward to each week and knew that they had not been forgotten. They were not "out of sight, out of mind."

Perhaps there would have been too many for a similar type service for all of the Methodist or Baptist patients. The only service I recall for all patients at the hospital was the annual Christmas service when gift packages were delivered to each patient.

At this time, Georgia had started building regional hospitals at Savannah, Columbus, Augusta, Rome, and Atlanta. In addition, the federal government was encouraging the establishment of community mental health centers. However, none of these were in place in Georgia in 1964 and 1965.

This vast hospital had its own water system and supplied much of the water to the surrounding community. Water was cheap if you had hospital water. There were no water meters. A person could let the water run 24 hours a day with no increase in the water bill. It was the same for staff housing on hospital grounds. There were no electricity meters and some staff let their air conditioners run full blast even when they were away on vacation.

That waste was not stopped until several years later when I worked in the Governor's Office of Planning and Budget (OPB). Staff could buy medications at the central pharmacy at very low cost and security at the pharmacy was lax. This was proven when Neil Jackson and I visited the hospital as employees of the Governor's Office of Planning and Budget. We simply walked into the back unlocked pharmacy door. Actually, it was more like a warehouse than a pharmacy.

Many of the hospital maintenance staff held second jobs as carpenters, painters, electricians, and so forth. They often drove old trucks that looked very similar to the hospital vehicles and parked their vehicles next to the state hospital vehicles. It was easy to "borrow" tools and equipment from one maintenance truck and toss it into their vehicles. Although there was a separate and marked parking place for employees' vehicles, they were seldom used, but I made a point of telling the commissioner of the Department of Human Resources what we knew was happening.

A security guard was finally caught stealing gasoline. He had a hog farm and a specially-equipped van with a 100-gallon tank in it. After locking the gates on the fenced-in area on Sunday mornings, he would cut off the gas pumps and proceed to fill the tank in the van. It was only after months of investigation and knowing that gasoline was being taken and not accounted for that the GBI was called in. The agent hid in a nearby building and watched. The GBI agent caught the security guard pumping gas into his 100-gallon tank in the van.

As the hospital population was dispersed to the regional hospitals and as community mental health centers were opened, it still required years of sustained effort to whittle the hospital budget down to a decent size.

During the 15 months we lived at Milledgeville, I served in the following buildings: Rivers building, a male unit where all patients wore khaki shorts and trousers; Veterans buildings; Arnall building, female receiving unit; main administration building, male receiving ward; Kemper building, female prisoners; and Binion building, psychiatric prisoners. Most buildings were named after former state public officials, except the Talmadges refused to allow a building to be named after them.

I worked with a variety of patients; however, I was never assigned to a mental retardation unit. During this time, the mentally retarded were largely ignored and lived in big open and true snake pit units. This was to change dramatically in a few short years with strong lobbying groups, sheltered workshops, and group homes in the communities.

Fellow interns with me were Henry Canzenera, Harold Newton, Mel Bonner, and Doug Fullington. Supervisors were Chappell Wilson, Henry Close, and Doug Turley.

The chaplain intern program was a tremendous learning experience for me with lectures with only four or five in a class, ward visits, verbatim reports on counseling sessions with patients, and review of reports. There was a constant reinforcing of observations of patient behavior by class critique and lectures plus library reading.

For the rest of the family, Milledgeville was a different kind of experience. Clarice worked in the Baldwin County Hospital operating room. Donna and Frank were in high school and Susan in an elementary school located near our home. Susan had an accident with a school yard gate and broke a front tooth that cost us, and then her, a great deal of money over the years.

Susan and Donna made friends with a neighbor, Mr. Farr, who had several horses and they were often invited to ride with him. It was there that they both learned to ride and love horses. For a brief time in Monticello we had owned a Shetland pony that Mr. Percy Pope gave the children as a Christmas present. The pony was a lot of trouble and we had sold him after a year or two. In the late 1990s, Donna and Susan visited Mr. Farr who had befriended them so often. He remembered them and was glad to see them again.

During the year we were in Milledgeville, I also served as pastor of Powelton Baptist Church in Hancock County, a very isolated rural church and one of the oldest in the state.

Although I did not use the counseling training in later years, the time at Milledgeville was an invaluable experience when I worked in the Governor's Office of Planning and Budget. I knew hospital routine and I knew questions to ask that would never occur to other budget staff members. One of my assignments during all the years I was in OPB was the Mental Health and Mental Retardation Division of the Department of Human Resources. I also knew something of the waste and dehumanizing that can happen when staff and administration are constantly thinking more of themselves than the well-being of the patients.

I remember the first communion service we held in the main chapel. Some of the patients reminded me of how I imagined the peasants in the Middle Ages as they came to worship. They had a true sense of awe and wonder on their faces as they knelt before the rail to receive communion. Perhaps it was one of the few times, or the only time, that they were being recognized as unique individuals and important in the eyes of God.

A few years later, I was to visit the old Central State Hospital at Milledgeville on a regular basis, but in a different capacity. By then the Regional Hospitals were in operation and the mental population at Milledgeville was down from 12,000 to around 3,500, but still a large hospital. The support system was much too large. The central kitchen and laundry were designed to serve 20,000. There was some offsetting of the use of this excess capacity by contracting with the prison system, which by then was taking over some of the hospital buildings.

Naturally the hospital gave up their oldest, worse buildings first. I remember one that was so bad the staff and patients put plastic sheets on the first floor beds in the daytime to protect the cover from urine and human waste from leaking sewer lines from the second floor ceiling. This was one of the first buildings turned over to the prison system.

Federal courts would never allow prisoners to be housed under such conditions, but mental patients seemed to be held in less regard. The prison system carried the costs of rehabilitating the old buildings when it took over. Later the prison system began to occupy some of the newer buildings, but one of the best, the Arnall building, was used for an administration building.

During the time we were at Milledgeville in the early 1960s, the new staff and professional staff and professional training staff took off on weekends as often as possible for Atlanta. The Jasper County police officers routinely caught a number of them for speeding through the county.

# War on Poverty

## 1965 - 1970

At the end of my chaplain intern period in the fall of 1965, it was time to find another job. Harold Newton and I were assured of employment with the Georgia Department of Education in the Vocational Rehabilitation Unit. Harold accepted a position with this agency, but I felt that I needed a job with more income.

Although I had considered some kind of counseling job, there were not many prospects. I do remember someone from the Home Mission Board flying down from Atlanta to give me a brief interview -- mainly to tell me that there were no job openings. I thought he was only out for an excuse to fly his plane for an hour or two.

I next turned to some of my friends who shared my views on religion and social issues. Will Campbell suggested I come to Tennessee. The War on Poverty was beginning and I was promised a job with the Tennessee Office of Economic Opportunity. However, there was a catch, it would be several months before they could start employment for me. As I could not wait, Clarice and I then drove across Tennessee and into North Carolina where our friend Heslip "Happy" Lee was executive director of the Salisbury-Rowan County Community Service Council.

North Carolina was one of the very first states to start the War on Poverty. In fact it was started under the guidance of Governor Terry Sanford before the federal government passed the anti-poverty bill. North Carolina had another advantage in that several millions of dollars had been obtained from the Ford Foundation in addition to state dollars. Thus with the big infusion of federal dollars, North Carolina was able to start many programs that later became models for other states.

### Salisbury-Rowan County Community Service Council

Happy Lee took me on as director of Manpower Development. My job was to write a proposal that would locate workers and train them for employment in the Piedmont section of North Carolina. The only problem was that the local board of directors was not too keen on the idea as the economy was quite strong in central North Carolina. It was the far eastern and the more western, mountainous parts of the state where jobs were scarce and folks were having a hard time making ends meet. However, the salary and benefits were good and we did move to Salisbury and were fortunate to be near our friends the Lees.

I made friends with several of the staff members including Hoyt Snipes, who later came to Georgia and worked with me in the Georgia Office of Economic Opportunity.

Happy Lee was a hard worker and expected as much from the rest of his staff, which was quite large. One winter day in 1966 there was a big snow storm and most roads were closed. Hoyt, Joe J. and I were the only three who made it to the office. There was no heat in the old former school building and most schools and businesses were closed. Happy had been away on a trip to West Virginia. He came back late in the day to find only the three of us at work and became very upset. "I came all the way from West Virginia and got to work, why did all the others fail to come in?" he demanded. We tried to explain to him that with no heat in the building it was not likely that much work would be done if folks did come in and we suggested folks stay home. Happy later took the three or four of us to lunch as some kind of reward for working the day when no other employees came in. He said we were the ones he could trust and depend on.

As the board was rather cool toward my manpower development program, I was soon looking for another job. Fortunately a new program was being established only a few miles west in Statesville, Iredell County, NC. Happy recommended me for the job and I was employed as executive director of Iredell County Action Research and Evaluation (I-CARE).

## Iredell County Action Research and Evaluation

In the fall we moved to Statesville and Frank became a freshman at Mercer University. This was again a time of change for the family, but a big challenge and an opportunity for me.

It was my job to hire and train staff, write grant applications, speak to groups, and meet regularly with board members. Very soon I had secretaries, director of Neighborhood Youth Corps, Vista volunteers, and a deputy director – a large staff to do great things.

One goal was the establishment of neighborhood service centers. We started two: one in Statesville and one in Mooresville. In addition, we had a summer Head Start program that was headed by the superintendent of the Mooresville Public School System.

I-CARE exhibit at Iredell County fair, Statesville, NC, 1967.

The local newspaper was the biggest thorn in my flesh. The editor had no use for the War on Poverty and seemed to be against almost anything that seemed to help folks in need.

There were two major towns in the county and one smaller town. The town of Love Valley in northern Iredell County was somewhat of an enigma. Andy Barker was mayor of Love Valley and a member of the board of I-CARE. He had built a western movie set cowboy town as a kind of permanent entertainment center. He was most anxious to get any kind of federal help he could. He had in prior months received some Ford Foundation money through the North Carolina Fund and was anxious for some Neighborhood Youth Corps programs or any other federal money he could get. He wanted me to visit his town, which I did. Then he insisted on giving me a pair of cowboy boots. I felt it was a bribe and insisted on paying for them but he refused to take my money. I always regretted taking the boots and I doubt that I wore them very often.

The town of Mooresville was totally different. The school principal, as I have stated, was a strong supporter of the Head Start program, Youth Corps program, Vista and Community Service Centers. It was always a pleasant experience to visit Mooresville.

My biggest problem proved to be with the regional Community Action Agency director from Washington, DC, where our regional office was located. He made it a point to visit our project very soon after we started the program. He then proceeded to tell the board that he was very disappointed in our Neighborhood Youth Corps program, a program of U.S. Department of Labor and nothing to do with his area of responsibility.

We did have more positions for this program and more money than we had requested in our grant application. When I took the application to the U.S. Department of Labor office in Washington, the reviewing officer promptly crossed out the number of positions requested and doubled it and then proceeded to double the amount of money I had requested. Remember, this was in the very early days of the War on Poverty, and it is my guess that the Washington decision makers dared not return any of the grant money to the federal treasury.

I had to establish two bank accounts in the local bank. One for U.S. Department of Labor funds and the other for Office of Economic Opportunity (OEO) funds. They were never to be mingled together. It was only later that I learned the Washington Economic Opportunity director wanted a black person in my position at I-CARE, and was quite willing to use any means fair or foul to see that I was removed from the office.

The local board of I-CARE thought I was doing a good job and told me so, however, they were all newcomers to the program and I guess they felt they had to listen to the man who held the purse strings. At any rate I resigned in December of 1967 in a move that was somewhat of a surprise to the board.

Several years later, the regional office was transferred to Atlanta and I was then working in the Georgia Office of Economic Opportunity. The regional Community Action Agency director from my NC days and I were both in a meeting. He was sounding off on some of his crusades and I had an opportunity to call his bluff and reminded him that I remembered him from my experience with him at Statesville. He had little impact on Georgia and soon left his position.

We had blacks in executive positions in the Georgia OEO office and, increasingly, in state government as "Ole" Lester Maddox operated a bit differently as governor than when he had operated his Pick Rick Restaurant in Atlanta.

Back in Statesville the black community split after I left for Atlanta. My deputy director, a fine black man with military administrative training, became the new director. One group changed the locks and kept the others out. The black community leaders were in a power struggle. The locked-out group picketed the I-CARE office. The resolution of the struggle was that the black director who followed Happy Lee at Salisbury went to I-CARE in Statesville and my former deputy director became the director of the Salisbury-Rowan Community Service Council.

I recall only one or two incidents of work with children in the I-CARE program. One was a little boy in the summer Mooresville Head Start program. The boy had terrible rotten teeth and we used Head Start money to have a dentist take care of him. The Mooresville principal invited me to go with him to take the boy home. The boy talked up a storm, but we could not understand a word he said. Then I asked him if he was going to get a bicycle for Christmas. His quick reply was, "She-it No!" This young white boy's vocabulary was clear and strong about some things.

The other was a teenage black girl in the Neighborhood Youth Corps program who flatly refused to do any work. I was asked to talk to her. Her defense was, "I ain't gonna wash no dishes." She had been assigned to help in the lunchroom. I told her she would soon be away from home and on her own and would have to clean her house, and so forth. I then asked her what she planned to be when she grew up. Her reply was, "I'm gonna be a fashion model." So much for that. Then she was assigned to be a teacher's aide and I think she did OK.

I was not good at public relations, putting articles in the paper, taking pictures, or speaking to civic and church groups. All were necessary in a public, tax-supported program and especially a new program in a community with a hostile press. Happy Lee did a far better job than I in that regard.

## Atlanta 1968, State Office of Economic Opportunity

Immediately after resigning from I-CARE, I drove to Atlanta and started looking for a job. The family stayed in Statesville to finish the school year.

I checked with Jim Parham, Director, Atlanta Office of Economic Opportunity. He had no openings and as I looked about his office, it seemed to be loaded with people who had Masters degrees in social work, as did Jim. My next search was to the federal regional labor department office. This looked promising with a possible job in a few weeks. However, I needed a job As Soon As Possible!

Next I checked into the Georgia Office of Economic Opportunity (OEO). E. C. Bryant was director and Al Dempsey was deputy director. E. C. was a bit slow about offering me a job, but when I told him about my background in North Carolina with their War on Poverty and about the possibility of a job with the U.S. Department of Labor, I was hired as training officer.

It so happened that I was the only person in the office who had direct experience in working in two Economic Opportunity programs at the local level. Georgia under Governor Lester Maddox was very slow getting started. Also, Georgia was under some pressure to get started as money allocated to a given state but not claimed could quickly be shifted to another state, such as North Carolina, that could absorb it.

It was a very good experience for me, traveling about the state explaining the program to new staff, new board members, and to labor department staff and local departments of Family and Children Services. The Georgia OEO was in fact, placed administratively under the Georgia Director of Family and Children Services, Bill Burson, who later became a very close friend of mine.

The state OEO office had a large staff of some twelve or more people. This contrasted with North Carolina that had only three people at the state level. Later, I was able to help Hoyt Snipes get a job with the state OEO office and also George Fields – Hoyt, because of his experience with the Salisbury-Rowan Community Service Council and George because he was a competent, committed, and very capable person. Both George and Hoyt continued to work in state government until they retired.

In traveling around the state, I met most of the directors of the anti-poverty programs. I met Frank Hill in Gainesville, where he served as an assistant director. He later served in our present home, Jasper, GA, as director of the program for this area, one of the better-operated programs that continues to have good local support. In fact, it was directed to take over another program that fell into severe criticism because of poor management.

One of the programs offered here in Jasper is the Mountain Area Transportation System (MATS) program. The director has had a strong transportation program in this area for some 20 years. I also worked with Frank a number of years ago on one of the state transportation committees.

The Georgia program was just getting underway when I was employed in the state office. However, I worked in that office only about nine months before I received a call from Bill Burson. I was visiting an employment office in North Georgia when he called me and offered me a job as director of the Department of Welfare's Public Information Office. This group had a staff of about five or six people and was located out on Peachtree Road. So my office moved from Marietta Street to Peachtree Road out near Lennox Square.

Bill Burson had regular meetings with his immediate staff. There were three or four of us at these meetings: his chief fiscal officer, chief program officer, and one other person whose duties I am unsure about. I was expected to attend also. Perhaps we were his listening device to keep him fully informed about what was going on in his domain and around the state. Bill was into politics in a big way, preparing to run for state treasurer.

Part of the responsibilities of my staff was to drive Bill around the state for his many speaking engagements. No matter how far away they went, Bill wanted and expected to be back in his office bright and early the next morning. His principal driver and my dear friend Paul Boring often had to drive until 2 AM or later getting back. Then Paul had to drive on home to Canton. Several times, I insisted that Paul stay home and rest after one of those long trips.

My immediate predecessor Geneva Brooks refused to drive Bill to some of his late appointments and he fired her and immediately offered me her job, which I accepted. Most of my staff used a slide show program to explain the work and various programs of the welfare department. Thus they too were on the go quite a lot.

Another of my duties was to serve as advisor to the Georgia Youth Council. This group was set up when Carl Sanders was governor. Most of the young people were bright, intelligent people and most were quite interested in Georgia politics. I remember some of the Georgia Youth Council and I met with Hubert Humphrey at Glenn Memorial Chapel on the Emory Campus when he was running for president in 1968.

Jimmy Carter abolished this group as soon as he became Governor, and I certainly approved of that. Money was used from the welfare department to pay for the hotel rooms and meals of the group when it met, usually in Atlanta.

My involvement in the War on Poverty led me along a number of pathways. All were interesting and educational and all prepared me for my extended years of service in the Governor's Office of Planning and Budget.

## Family Memories of Statesville

Our family's most memorable leisure times while living in Statesville were weekend trips to various sections of the Blue Ridge Parkway. For Donna, a life-long love of the Parkway developed. Earlier when we lived at Monticello, we had traveled up the Parkway to Canada, tent-camping along the way.

One summer Frank Lonnie and a friend of his left Statesville and went to Illinois to work on a Campbell's soup farm. We were upset because he did not write. We finally tracked him down through the family of his friend.

Our 1966 Christmas letter contained the following report of some of our activities:

> ...an exceedingly busy and active life this year... visited community programs in New Haven, CT, one of the most successful job training programs in the nation. Other trips to Temple University in Philadelphia, Washington, DC. Chapel Hill, NC, Atlanta, and the Institute of Government at the University of North Carolina.
>
> Frank enrolled at Mercer University this fall after graduating with honors at Boyden High School in Salisbury and spending the summer working as a truck driver, field hand, belt fixer, car hop, and traveling salesman.
>
> During the summer, Clarice and I made a trip to Atlanta, where I had been invited to lecture on the role of a minister in a Community Action Program. This was at Emory University for the annual summer Church and Community Workshop that I had attended several times in prior years.
>
> When asked about leaving the ministry my reply was, "God can call folks into the preaching pulpit ministry and he can call them out."

The calling is no less real and meaningful. This, in addition, is a calling to a kind of ministry that the average, comfortable middle class Protestant church has largely ignored.

"For the needy will not always be forgotten, nor the hope of the afflicted perish forever." Psalms 9:18

Following Donna's graduation from high school, the family moved to Decatur, Georgia.

# Prayer in the Midst of Change

## May 20, 1978

O God, we are still today a pilgrim people. Like sheep we are ready to nibble away our time, energy, and resources until there is none left.

We are finite, frail human beings, subject to many moods, influences, and the constant invasions of our privacy and of our being – unless Thou doest fill us with Thy love, hope and an inner sense of direction, meaning and purpose we will surely roll to and fro like the tumbleweeds, storm-tossed with no roots to stand or to grow.

Help me to lower my defenses of fear of being hurt and risk the tumult of change and, finally, help me to know Thy presence in the midst of change.

Amen.

# Hedonists

"Rugged individualists," we Americans like to call ourselves. Meanwhile we rugged individuals drive along in our oversized chariots with our eyes and C. B. "ears" on the lookout for "Smokey" and well aware that we are driving over the speed limit. Thus, we consume and waste the drops of fossil fuel that are now being wrung from beneath the desert sands of the Middle East and the vast areas beneath the frozen seas.

In reality, we are but dependent cocoons: fetuses in our automobile wombs with umbilical cords that stretch around the world and under the seas. One of these days, these lifelines will surely dry up and we rugged individuals will indeed become squalling brats.

# Four Governors

## 1968 – 1988

Between the years 1968 and 1988, I had the unique opportunity to work fairly closely with four governors: Lester Maddox, Jimmy Carter, George Busbee, and Joe Frank Harris.

Although not directly assigned to Lester Maddox's office while he served as governor, I did see him from time to time and as advisor to the Governor's Youth Council, I met with him on occasion. During the Carter, Busbee, and Harris administrations, I served in the Governor's Office of Planning and Budget (OPB) and therefore did see these men rather frequently during the governor's review and preparation of the governor's budget in the fall months. The four were vastly different people with different interests and different personalities.

### Lester Maddox (Governor 1967 – 1971)

Lester Maddox delegated a lot of administrative duties to his administrative assistant Zell Miller, and thus I also came to know Zell a number of years before he, too, became governor and then senator.

Lester had some very strong ideas that he pushed and later fought Jimmy Carter throughout the Carter Administration. This was because Lester got himself elected lieutenant governor after having served as governor. Lieutenant Governor Lester Maddox was presiding officer of the Georgia Senate, a powerful position from which to throw road blocks at Carter.

However, Lester did have his own way of being a showman. During one Christmas season, he proceeded to put on a Santa Claus uniform and visit state employees on the street around the capitol building and various state office buildings. In fact I have a color photo taken on the sidewalk in front of one of the state office buildings where I, along with others, visited with Governor "Santa" Maddox.

On one occasion, during a Georgia Youth Council meeting with Maddox, the young people had very little opportunity to share with the governor their interests, views and desires for Georgia's future. Maddox seized the opportunity to give a long lecture on what he thought his Youth Council should be doing for him and promoting his agenda.

Actually, the Georgia Youth Council was established by Carl Sanders when he was governor. Youth were selected from each congressional district and youth who were expected to have some interests and commitment to Georgia government and with leadership potential. Bill Burson, the director of the state welfare department, was my immediate boss during this time. Burson called the Youth Council a "cheering section" for Carl Sanders. I suppose neither Maddox or his successor Jimmy Carter had any love for Sanders as he was their political rival. The Youth Council was abolished shortly after Carter became governor.

Zell Miller on one occasion, called George Fields and me into his office. I never knew exactly why the two of us were singled out to meet with him, other than the fact that we both had some experience in and perhaps some ability to write grant proposals for federal money.

Francis giving unsolicited advice to Zell MIller when Zell was running for reelection as governor in the fall of 1994.

This was exactly what Zell, and supposedly Maddox, wanted from us. The grant request was to the U.S. Department of Labor for a youth employment director. George and I put our heads together and I used some of the buzz words that I knew would appeal to the decision makers in

Washington. George wrote the application and his dear wife, Nell typed it up.

The application was forwarded to Washington and the grant was made to the state. Later George and I received a commendation from Zell in which he said Washington said it was one of the very best applications submitted. The only hitch was that the money was only enough to hire one staff person and allow that person some travel money. There was no money for kids to be employed.

However, Barry Reid was the person employed and he turned out to be a great asset to the state where he later served as director of the Governor's Office of Consumer Affairs. He held that position for a number of years. Barry also became a close friend of many of us in state government. In fact Barry worked in Carter's office as Carter was establishing his Office of Planning and Budget and, in turn, Barry asked me to serve under him as senior planner in the Human Development Division, which I was glad to do.

### Jimmy Carter (Governor, 1971 – 1975)

In contrast to Maddox, Jimmy Carter was very much a "hands on" governor. This was both Carter's strength and weakness, especially after he became President of the USA. Carter was indeed a dedicated, strong-willed and committed governor. Carter's background was as a state senator, farmer, businessman, and Navy officer in the submarine service. As an engineer, he was interested in the inner-operating details of state agencies.

Carter grappled with the idea of "zero-based budgeting." Every state agency in its budget request was to justify every position and every proposed expenditure, every year. The net result was a vast mountain of paper hauled into the Governor's Office of Planning and Budget that simply overwhelmed the governor and his OPB "bean counters." The idea of zero-based budgeting sounds great, but in practice there are better ways of doing budgets and, to my knowledge, there were no further state attempts at zero-based budgeting.

Carter was an early bird at the Governor's Office. I also went in early to eat breakfast before the 8 AM work hour. Frequently I would see Carter coming in at 7 AM and I am sure he often came in earlier than 7 AM However, he left around 5 PM.

There are one or two interesting stories about Carter that to my knowledge never received any publicity. One early morning Carter called Steve Polk into his office. Steve was the head of what became the Office of

Administrative Services and was responsible for all maintenance of state office buildings.

To Steve's amazement, Carter led Steve into the governor's private bathroom and showed him several rolls of stacked up toilet paper. Carter then began lecturing Steve and informing him that he had calculated the number of bathrooms in state offices and using the figure he found in his bathroom projected that far and away too much toilet paper was being placed in bathrooms where it might be stolen. At any rate, it was a costly and unnecessary expense. Steve immediately issued an order to cut back on state employees toilet paper.

Early one morning, I had occasion to be in Carter's office and noted a log on the table behind the governor's desk. The log was draped with Spanish moss. The center piece in front of the log was a very large soft-shell snapping turtle with its head against the center of the log. We asked the governor where it came from. Carter informed us that "Mr. Ben" had brought it in to him a few minutes earlier.

I could not wait to see Mr. Ben Fortson, Secretary of State, and find out what his gift to the governor was all about. Ben Fortson's office was only a few steps down the hall from the governor's office and Ben in his wheel chair was always the very first person one met when he stepped in the door. Later Governor Busbee commented that Mr. Ben would have his desk in the hall if he could get away with it. Mr. Ben was always the greeting, hand-shaking politician. At any rate, I asked Mr. Ben about his gift to the governor. He laughed and said, "That big ole swamp snapping turtle is Carter. It is too stubborn to go over, around or under the log, but if you will look closely, it has a little hole drilled into the log and that is just like Carter. He will keep pushing his nose into the log until he drills a hole through it."

Needless to say, it did not stay in Carter's office very long. It would be great to have it displayed at the Carter Center, but I doubt if it will and I don't know what Carter ever did with it.

Ben Fortson had been in charge of the capitol grounds and property until Carter became governor. At that time Carter established the Department of Administrative Services and put Steve Polk, a former state highway patrol officer, in charge. Carter did like Steve. Steve himself was a great storyteller and once told a good story on Mr. Ben Fortson.

Mr. Fortson had called Steve into his office, shortly after Steve took over Ben Fortson's old job as keeper of the state office buildings. Fortson proceeded to "bless Steve out for some housekeeping infraction," to use Steve's words. Steve burst out laughing at Mr. Ben. Fortson became quite irritated at Steve's response and asked him what was so funny. Steve said, "I can hardly wait to get home to talk to my momma." "And why is that?" Mr. Ben asked.

Steve replied, "I am going to tell her that I have just been "blessed out" by the Secretary of State of Georgia, and I know she will feel pleased and honored." Ben had to laugh and that ended the encounter.

Carter served only four years as governor, but in reality, he was running for U.S. President during his last two years as governor. He had sent his top lieutenant Hamilton Jordan to serve in a high staff position on the Democratic National Committee. Hamilton, as his chief political strategist, was able to make necessary contacts and lay out the plan for his national campaign. I remember that early on, one part of Carter's strategy was to ask his staff to give him suggestions on how to deal with inner-city poverty.

I sent him a clipping from the Smithsonian Magazine about inner-city flower and vegetable gardens on vacant city lots. The gardens were well tended and not vandalized. Carter, a farmer, could relate to that and sent me a note of thanks.

Carter naturally made a lot of enemies in the Georgia General Assembly and around the state as he, like Mr. Ben's turtle, pushed very hard to bring about much needed and constructive changes in state government.

However, many of the changes he made have been changed again. The Department of Offender Rehabilitation under Carter was later changed back to the Department of Corrections. The Division of Youth Services and several other divisions of the Department of Human Resources were later spun off into separate departments. But then change of agency titles seems to be the nature of government. When folks balk at taxes and the problem refuses to disappear, it is easier to simply make a lot of noise and change the name of the agency.

I had a unique opportunity to see Carter at work first hand. On one occasion, during the budget development process he asked for a report on the Department of Corrections reorganization plan. Remember, Carter was great on planning. I had been a member of the task force working on this plan, but I was not a major player. I had to tell him that the plan was not complete. Carter became quite upset and said, "I have reorganized state government in far less time than this." He immediately proceeded to write a note to Commissioner Ellis McDougal telling him that he needed the plan As Soon As Possible. I was amused the next day to get a phone call from the department's chief planning officer informing me that the planning trip to

Savannah had been cancelled as it was now time to turn in the plan. That planning officer did not last much longer in state government.

Another staff member in the Governor's Office of Planning and Budget who did not last long, resulted in a lot of amusement on the part of other staff members. Carter always had the OPB staff come to his office. The result was that some 10 or 15 staff members would walk a couple of blocks carrying many volumes of budget information for the governor. One morning the group had been sitting quietly saying nothing with Governor Carter saying nothing. Finally, in walked the tardy staff person, carrying a cup of coffee in his hand and with no apology for being late or keeping the governor waiting. This was almost an unpardonable sin in Carter's view. That staff member soon disappeared from the grounds of the state capitol.

On another occasion, some of the budget staff were meeting with the governor during the lunch hour. Carter, ever the busy man, was working through lunch hour and had his lunch brought in with not even a coke for the rest of us. Carter, a very religious man, bowed his head in silent prayer before eating his meal. Battle Hall, acting commissioner of the newly organized Department of Human Resources, was in a big hurry to start his pitch for money and failed to note that Carter was praying. Battle Hall continued to talk all the time Carter was praying. Again, another career in state government was cut short, and Battle went back to Floyd county to continue his accounting business.

Carter, a serious man, did have a light moment or two that he shared with us. I well remember one joke he told:

> A Divinity student was reading his Bible quietly in the college dining hall. An extremely beautiful and well-endowed young woman came up and asked if she could sit across the table from him and the divinity student quietly invited her to be seated.
>
> She engaged in small talk for a few moments and then got up and in a very loud voice so that other students could hear, said "OK. I'll see you in my room." The divinity student was very embarrassed and turned red in the face.
>
> The young woman then sat back down and said, "I'm a psychology major and I'm testing students' reactions to my statement." To which the divinity student, in a very loud voice replied, "Fifty Dollars!"

As a planner and not a budget analyst, at the time, it was part of my job to develop quantifiable, measurable performance measures on each agency assigned to me. The agencies included Workers Compensation, Labor Department, Offender Rehabilitation, and Mental Health (mostly hospitals, but later community mental health programs as well as hospitals). I doubt that members of the House and Senate appropriations committees ever spent much time looking at performance measures, but Carter wanted them and they were included in every budget document submitted by the governor and by succeeding Governors Busbee and Harris.

Still later, the OPB staff were combined and we were all given the new title of Policy Analyst.

Both Governors Busbee and Harris had a better plan for reviewing budget submissions. They came over to our office to work on the budget. This took the governor away from his immediate staff and away from interruptions from people who simply had to see the governor for a minute or two. Also, it resulted in better use of our staff time as we could wait in our office and continue working until four or five minutes before it was our turn to meet with the governor.

However, before we presented our recommendations to the governor, we first had to make our presentation to the division director and then the office director. This procedure had a two-fold purpose: one, to make sure that we had our facts and figures together and presented in a short, clear, concise manner, and two, to help these two individuals have a clear understanding of what we were recommending.

Later, after we met with the governor, he in turn would meet with the department heads, but we would be in the room with the governor at this time. After the department heads made their presentation we would remain with the governor for a few minutes and make any final recommendations or suggestions we wished to present. Thus the Office of Planning and Budget staff had a powerful role in helping the governor shape his budget recommendation that he would present to the General Assembly in January.

When Carter was elected President and went up to Washington, quite a few of his staff went with him. Hamilton Jordan, Jody Powell, Bert Lance, and Jim McIntyre are perhaps the best known. However, there were others – Jack Kelley and several others from the Office of Planning and Budget. One reporter later asked if Carter brought all of his Georgia staff to Washington. Jody's reply was, "No, only the dumb ones." Jim Parham went up to serve as an under secretary in the U.S. Department of Health,

Education and Welfare. However, Jim and several others soon decided that Georgia was a better place than Washington.

Here's one final story about Carter and his staff. Tom Linder, grandson of a former Commissioner of Agriculture, was chosen by Carter to head up his new Office of Planning and Budget. Tom had been director of an Area Planning and Development Commission in middle Georgia and perhaps had some military experience. Tom was director of the office when I was first employed in that agency. Part of the ritual was to go in and meet the man. His main shot at me was that we were to work very hard and be prepared to work many long hours. My reply was that I was raised on a farm working long hours and that a seven day week and 365-days-a-year job was nothing new or difficult for me. That seemed to please him.

About the time I was employed, Tom decided that a GI, military-style work party was in order. Staff were to report for duty on a weekend and proceed to give the entire office a thorough cleaning. This despite the fact that an army of workers came into all the state offices every week night to clean and vacuum as necessary. At any rate, a number of employees reported on the appointed Saturday for work. However, one employee tipped off a newspaper reporter, and that made a great story the next day along with a cartoon on the editorial page of employees on their hands and knees scrubbing floors. The GI party backfired on the "can do" Linder and he, too, was soon working away in private business.

## George Busbee (Governor 1975 – 1983)

Before being elected governor, George Busbee had served for a number of years in the Georgia House of Representatives, and finally as Chairman of the Appropriations Committee, one of the most powerful positions next to that of Speaker of the House. George was very much the insider as opposed to Carter. He was not intimidated by Mr. Ben, as was Carter. Carter seemed to defer to older officials, but not Busbee. When Ben Fortson came in to make his pitch for money to Busbee, Busbee had placed some kind of freeze on state spending. When he was turned down, Mr. Ben immediately spun his wheel chair around and sped out of the meeting room.

Busbee did defer to Tom Murphy. In fact, Tom was the major player in helping Busbee to be elected. I had been the most knowledgeable person on both Carter's and Busbee's staffs in the area of mental health. First, because I had worked for over a year in the state hospital at Milledgeville, and second, I had been assigned to visit both the state hospitals and the very few federally funded community mental health and mental retardation programs.

I pointed out to James Mackey, a former congressman and close friend and advisor to Busbee, that our state had few mental retardation programs and a state law supporting mental retardation programs, but no law or support for community programs for the alcoholics, drug abusers, and mentally ill. Mackey saw that this was an idea whose time had come. His response to me was, "In this millennium! A bureaucrat who knows something about both the law, mental health programs, and what to do about them." He was surprised that such an idea came from a bureaucrat. It was time to get the ball rolling on community mental health programs.

I pressured my supervisor in the initial budget review process and later the director of the Office of Planning and Budget to push the governor in establishing a pilot alcohol treatment program. Both refused the request but suggested that I take it directly to Governor Busbee, which I did. Busbee's reply was that he would do it, but Tom Murphy was going to shoot it down, because he hates drunks and will have nothing to do with it. This is exactly how it played out the first year.

However, we came back the second year, after there had also been increased local support across the state and from the General Assembly, and the pilot program was established in Griffin. By the time I left state government in 1988, alcohol treatment programs, drug treatment programs, and community mental health centers were pretty well established in a network across the state. This could not have happened during the Carter administration, even though his wife was and continues to be a very strong advocate for better and more humane treatment for the mentally ill. Carter had made too many enemies during his four years as governor.

When Busbee became governor, there were only two state-funded alcohol treatment centers in the state. One was in Savannah and the other in the old Asa Candler mansion on Briarcliff Road in Atlanta. Both were established way back when Herman Talmadge was governor, in the early 1950s. The regional hospitals had what were called 28-day alcohol treatment centers, but were costly to operate and federal funds and programs had been oriented away from hospitals and toward community programs since the 1960s.

However, Carl Sanders in the 1960s was busy with the big push for regional mental hospitals. This was in fact the follow-up to the great expose by Jack Nelson, the reporter for the Atlanta newspapers, in the very early

1960s of the terrible "snake pit" conditions that existed at the old Milledgeville State Hospital.

No doubt, similar conditions existed in many state run hospitals around the nation. The federal government was pushing for better prevention and treatment programs at the community level at the very time Georgia was spending millions on brick and mortar buildings: Rome, three in the Atlanta area, Columbus, Augusta, Savannah, and later Bainbridge. Later in the 1990s, two of the hospitals in Atlanta were closed. One was turned over to DeKalb county and the old Georgia Mental Health Institute was turned over to Emory University.

Busbee was a much more laid-back governor than was Carter. Carter was a very intense person who wanted to get it done now and get it over with, besides he had his eye on Washington in only a few months after he became governor. After all, how many governors have their picture on the front cover of Time magazine in a very short time after being installed in office?

Busbee could laugh about piloting a state plane (he had owned a plane in prior years) into Atlanta through a storm, late one night. He told us coming into Charlie Brown Airport against a powerful head wind, he said he cut the engine and dropped it in. This was a very dangerous stunt for a governor. I doubt that state pilots turned over the controls to him on any later flights.

Busbee seemed to enjoy being with his staff. He participated in a soft ball game with us out at Chastain Park and, on another occasion, invited the entire staff out to a Matt Dillon and Miss Kitty cowboy/cowgirl party at the governor's mansion. We were all dressed in our western outfits and we had our pictures made with the Busbees. I don't remember what the chow was, but I'm sure it was quite suitable for the occasion.

Old West banquet at the Governor's mansion. Left to right: Clarice Stewart, Gov. George Busby, Mary Beth Busby, Francis Stewart

Because Busbee was well liked in the General Assembly and generally well liked around the state, he was able to get a constitutional amendment passed that allowed governors to be elected to no more than two terms. Busbee, Harris, and Zell Miller all served two terms.

At the time of Busbee's second Inaugural Ball, I invited our daughter Susan to attend with me. She did get to meet him and hopefully had her picture made with Busbee at that time.

Budget reviews with Busbee were always carried out in a serious, but much more relaxed atmosphere than was the case with Carter.

## Joe Frank Harris (Governor 1983 – 1991)

Neither my journal nor my memory serve up much information about Joe Frank as governor. He was a very quiet man, a well-liked man. His father had been a leader in the Indian Springs Camp Ground summer religious gatherings. In his own way, I am sure he was as deeply spiritual as Jimmy Carter. However, he did not make any outward show of it. As did Busbee before him, Joe Frank came across the capitol grounds to the Trinity-Washington Building to meet with his OPB staff. Thus, we were spared having to carry arm loads of documents to his office for review.

I remember one joke he told on the Cartersville Baptists. He said no matter how hard they tried, the Methodists could never get more people to church on Sunday morning than the Baptists. So, one day the Methodists sent out a spy. The spy reported back that a parking lot attendant at the Baptist Church was the official counter. He further reported that the attendant was counting folks who passed by the church if they waved, but not if they passed the church and failed to wave. This was a sure way of beating the Methodists.

On one occasion, I attended a prayer breakfast downtown. I noticed Governor Harris sitting all alone at a table and I went over to visit with him. Later a woman came in who was an activist in the health field and came to the table reserved for her. I got up to leave but Harris insisted that I remain and I did. Later, I received a photo of the governor and me at that breakfast. I looked properly solemn and serious.

Gov. Joe Frank Harris and Francis Stewart at prayer breakfast.

By the time Harris was governor, I was looking forward to retirement and spending as much time as possible at Fernwood in Pickens County building the barn, working on the driveway, setting out many rhododendrons, native azaleas, evergreen azaleas, and other work as time allowed. I was also looking forward to a lot of attention to family.

## Flight Through a Hail Storm

On Friday, June 5, 1981, I flew to Augusta, leaving home at 6 AM and not getting back home until after 7 PM. As I was the only passenger on the State of Georgia plane, the pilot allowed me to sit in the cockpit with him on the return trip to Atlanta. We had to fly through some rather rough clouds plus hail and hard rain. The flight controller had attempted to route us around the thunderstorms to the safest available route. Our radar picked out the worst clouds and occasionally we would fly between the towering thunderheads. Since I was in the co-pilot's seat I could see and hear everything going on between the air traffic controller, tower, and the pilot.

It was quite an experience. Once we were ordered to descend to a lower altitude and the pilot attempted to comply and although the nose of the plane was pointed down the altimeter indicated we were in fact going up, such was the awesome power of the thermal updraft. At another report, the air traffic controller reported a plane under us and asked if we could see it. We reported in the negative as we could not see anything but rain and hail.

When we finally reached the Charlie Brown airport and the plane touched down to a safe landing, the pilot let out a deep and profound sigh of relief. And I, too, took a very deep breath and offered a silent prayer of thanksgiving.

## Make Your Voice Heard By Government

It was my privilege to work in the executive branch of Georgia state government and to observe first hand the work of many of the committees in the Georgia General Assembly. One of the main tasks of the Governor's Office of Planning and Budget staff is to provide an analysis of literally hundreds of bills, track each bill through committees of the House and Senate, analyze committee and floor amendments and substitutes, and attend hearings.

However, these are only some of the tasks to be performed. Much more time is needed to check proposed bills against existing state law. What is the exact nature of the change that will result? What is the purpose of the bill?

Who will benefit? In what way? Is this in accord with the legal mission of the state agency that will have to administer it? Who will it hurt? In what way? Finally, how much more is it going to cost or save the state?

Obviously this takes time. Especially as bills are amended or substituted, for this process as outlined above must be repeated in whole or in part with each change.

The literal flood of bills that seems to provide this group or that group some special benefits is enough to turn some people off. To me it merely confirms the best insights of the accumulated wisdom of man about man, wisdom and insights gathered across the span of man's recorded history: We want to help, but first of all, to help ourselves!

This should not be any surprise as we look at government in all its levels: local, state, and federal. And, as we look at all of our various and sundry business enterprises, we see that those who best know, understand, and use (or manipulate) the system, stand to gain the most from it.

Campaign finance reforms and consumer protection bills seem to have an especially hard time.

There are those who damn, blast, and curse government and there will always be these folks. However, in a society that is expanding its population at a very rapid rate and as more and more demands are being made for limited and finite resources of water, fossil fuel, land, and trees, it becomes ever more clear that it is of the utmost, urgent importance that we exercise far better stewardship of our scarce and finite resources. Thus, it falls on those we elect in our democracy to establish ever better ways and means to shepherd, preserve, and develop our finite resources of air, water, and land.

Over the past 45 years, thousands of acres of land and forests have been bulldozed to make way for our vast network of interstate and local highways. Whole neighborhoods have been displaced to make way for freeways, MARTA, shopping malls, warehouses, closely packed together residential areas, and so forth.

Land that was once farmland now sprouts acres of houses on tiny lots.

As folks are crowded together, where are the open spaces and green fields for children to play? Parents and neighbors have to shuttle their children to distant parks, playgrounds, and ball fields because there is no room for them to play close to home. In short, the small town life where every kid is known and every kid feels free to roam about the village no longer exists. What a shame!

# Desert Flowers

As guest pastor, I gave this sermon on June 15th, 1980, at Oakhurst Baptist Church in Decatur, Georgia, where Clarice and I were members.

Scripture:   I John 3:14 – 18

Text:   14 We know that we have passed out of death into life, because we love the brethren. He who does not love abides in death. 15 Any one who hates his brother is a murderer, and you know that no murderer has eternal life abiding in him.

16 By this we know love, that he laid down his life for us; and we ought to lay down our lives for the brethren. 17 But if any one has the world's goods and sees his brother in need, yet closes his heart against him, how does God's love abide in him? 18 Little children, let us not love in word or speech but in deed and in truth.

Theme:   There is more to life than seeing (far more than meets the eye), and there is more to ourselves, for good or evil, than most of us are willing or capable to admit.

## Introduction

Earl Loomis, in the opening chapter of his book *The Self in Pilgrimage*, tells about a remarkable story that decisively influenced his life.

Loomis tells of a farmer who saw a frightening vision in his barnyard. He saw his cows peacefully chewing their cuds, the hens clucking to their chicks, a lizard lazily sunning himself. Then suddenly the peaceful barnyard scene was transformed into a threatening jungle: The cows became dinosaurs, the chickens were vultures, the lizard became a python.

The dismaying scene lasted just a moment and then vanished. The placid scene of the cows, the hens and their chicks, and the lazy lizard returned. The farmer's terror subsided. But he never again looked on his barnyard creatures in the way he had before. From then on, he always wondered which was real: the domestic farm scene or the primitive wildness.

Loomis states that after that story, he began to wonder which was the "real me" – the way he imagined himself to be or the way he was in depth. He says that at last, he could begin to learn to know himself.

He thought he had known and plumbed his depths. But he discovered that most of the "real me" had been hiding from reality for years. He had worked at being good and avoiding evil, but had not confronted the fact that there were both good and evil within himself. He had tried to believe the right things and behave and feel in the right way. But he did not fully own the standards of "right."

All this began to change as he realized that if he were something other than what he thought he was, then perhaps he was composed of qualities he saw and despised in others. He began to wonder if he were selfish, vindictive, crude, lustful, jealous.

When he began to accept the possibility of these evil inner threats, he discovered something even more awesome and challenging. He realized that there were also aspects of his strengths that he had not known before.

Loomis says that from that moment on he knew with certainty that if he wanted to know the person he really was, he would have to accept both the good and the bad within himself.

## Journey to Death in the Desert

In life there are both things we want to see and believe and things we seemingly will go to any length to avoid seeing and believing.

As some of you know, a few weeks ago Clarice and I had the occasion to make our first trip to California and Nevada. We looked forward in great anticipation to visiting our children in Nevada and seeing that great desert and sky country that heretofore we had seen only on TV and in cowboy movies.

One day our daughter Susan and her friends took us across the desert some 30 miles to Virginia City, Nevada. As we traveled across the desert, Susan and her young friends pointed out the original narrow, twisting roads used by the wagon trains and stage coaches.

Later we were somewhat surprised to discover that Virginia City was not exactly what we expected to see; not an empty ghost town with empty buildings, swinging doors, creaking floors and no people, but rather a tourist sightseers' mecca and a series of shops and historical museums. Not exactly what we had imagined we would see.

We went out beyond the town's edge to the cemetery. The cemetery, located on a high desert plateau, was rimmed by treeless desert mountains. As we walked over the cemetery we came upon a grave with a wooden fence surrounding it and a wooden tombstone as a marker. At the head of the grave was a small tree, about the size of a dogwood, except that the tree was barren and lifeless.

At that point Clarice spoke and said, "Francis, get a picture of that tree. That says it all. Now that's Nevada!"

It is hard to imagine a greater contrast between that Nevada desert scene in the graveyard and our own dense green forests and woodlands of Georgia and the southeastern United States.

The next day Susan drove us even farther out into the desert to an Indian reservation. As we walked across the desert, we had time to examine the sand, tumbleweeds, rocks, and to discover a host of tiny, fragile looking desert flowers. Flowers that until we came upon them had surely "blushed unseen and wasted their sweetness on the desert air."[1]

Indeed we learned that there was far more in the dry, arid desert than that portion we saw in the Virginia City graveyard. Earlier, we made a short walk across the hot, dry sandy desert into an old 1861 silver mine. We were immediately struck with the contrast between the blazing noonday desert sun and the cool, quiet darkness of the mine, and yet the two were separated by only a few feet of soil. We were amazed at the amount of water dripping from overhead and running almost to our shoe tops on the floor of the mine shaft. Water and cool air only a few short yards from the hot noonday desert sun!

The current tissue of *Sojourner's* magazine has an excellent article on the transforming powers of the desert. During the Third Century some of the early Christians, following the example of Our Lord, frequently went out into the wilderness to find solitude and pray.

It is said that Anthony, known as Father of Monks, withdrew into the desert, where for twenty years he lived in complete solitude. During this twenty year span he experienced a terrible ordeal. His superficial, external shell was cracked and the abyss of iniquity was opened to him. He overcame

---

1. *Elegy in a Country Church Yard*, by Thomas Gray

this trial, not by his own power, but because of his unconditional surrender to the Lordship of Jesus Christ.

When he emerged from his solitude after twenty years, people recognized in him the real, "healthy" whole man. Whole in mind, body, and spirit. They flocked to him for comfort, direction, and healing.

The transformation to being centered in Jesus Christ came from solitude, the furnace where transformation took place. And it is from the transformed or converted, born again self that real ministry flows.

If you asked the Desert Fathers why solitude gives birth to compassion, they might say, "Because it makes us die to our neighbor."

At first, this answer seems quite disturbing to a modern mind. But when we give it a closer look, we can see that in order to be of service to others, we have to die to them. That is, we have to give up measuring our meaning of value by the yardstick of others. To die to our neighbors means to stop judging them, to stop evaluating them, and thus to become free to be compassionate. Compassion can never coexist with judgement, because judgement creates the distance, the againstness that prevents us from really being with the other person.

The Children of Israel pleaded and prayed to go back into slavery and bondage in Egypt. At least in Egypt they no longer had to deal with their own selfishness and inadequacies. For to them, the wilderness desert was a place of terror, wrath, thorns, plagues, desolation, weariness, thirst, and death. Better to die as a slave in Pharaoh's Egypt. For such a place forces one into a continuing encounter with one's innermost being and with God.

I doubt that we today have changed that much from the Children of Israel. We steer clear of the desert of silence and solitude. That desert wasteland of good and evil within our own selves, of which Earl Loomis wrote.

Carlyle Marney in his book *Faith in Conflict* writes, "Afraid of silence, we create a din. To avoid the threat of loneliness, we live in a crowd. Afraid of unemployment, we hire ourselves to death (our own Egypt land). Threatened by work, we become slaves to machinery. Aware of the dangers of isolation, we join everything. Shocked by old age, we camouflage with makeup. Searching for rest, we drive ourselves to frenzy... Seeking realization, we come up with nerves. Uncertain of peace, we prepare for war until finally and inevitably, the only thing left to do is fight!"

## To the Promised Land of Life, Hope, and Love

It was the shortest route from Egypt to the Promised Land for the Children of Israel. The shortest route, but it required forty years of travel and repentance to grow from freedom and idolatry to freedom and discipline under God. The transformation of the Ten Commandments from mere tablets of stone to laws of the heart required forty years and more before these rag-tag people became a people set apart and prepared to live as God's people.

Earlier I read I John 3:14 – 18. I want to read it again for you and paraphrase portions of it as I read.

We know that we have passed out of the desert of death and into the Promised Land of life, because we love the brethren. He that loveth not his brother, (*but is preoccupied with self and selfish gain*) abideth in the desert of death.

Whosoever hateth his brother is a murderer and you know that no murderer hath the Promised Land of eternal life abiding in him. Hereby perceive we the love of God, because he (*acted*) to lay down his life for us and we ought to lay down our lies for the brethren. (*That they might abide in the shadow of the mighty rock within the weary desert land and sheltered from the fierce storms of greed, hatred, and selfishness.*)

But he who has this world's goods and sees his brother in need and closes his heart to him, how does God's love abide in Him? (*He is as dry, arid, and dead as the wooden tombstone and dead tree in the Nevada desert.*)

My little children, let us not love in word, neither in tongue, but in deed and in truth.

Let Oakhurst be the Church out there, in Decatur, in Atlanta, in the Georgia Baptist Children's Home where Chris and Hazel Grady work, in the school where Dora McCullen teaches, the Fulton County Juvenile court, where Herb Snedden works, McKinney's Apothecary where Bill McKinney serves people who are sick. Let Oakhurst be the Church on West Howard street as well as here on East Lake Drive.

A few months before he was killed, and the last time I saw him alive, Martin Luther King Jr. was speaking at Johnson C. Smith University in Charlotte, NC. In the mind of the press, M. L. King was then in eclipse. Black Power was the word. Nonviolence seemed to be overtaken by a far more exciting theme in the eyes of the press and even in the minds of some of his followers.

At that time in his message when M. L. answered his critics, he responded this way, and this was the high point of his message:

> "They keep asking me, if I still believe in nonviolence. I want to assure you that even if some day I am the last man on earth who believes in nonviolence, I will still believe in nonviolence and will believe in it with every fiber of my being!"

Thus he stood as a towering giant of a rock among the swirling sands of confusion, unrest, bigotry, and hatred. Or, if you please, as a desert flower reflecting God's love in a wilderness of despair and hate. Yes, they killed the dreamer but they did not kill the dream!

Today we too stand at the crossroads. We have irrevocable choices to make and once made, we cannot go back and start over. As a pilgrim desert people, we know that there are those all about us who are searching for the wellsprings of hope in a troubled and dangerous land. The parable of the last judgement is ever before us, "I was hungry and you gave me food, I was thirsty and you gave me drink. I was a stranger and you welcomed me. I was naked and you clothed me. I was sick and you visited me. I was in prison and you came to me. ... As you did it unto the least of these my brethren, you did it to me."[2]

Last week I reviewed an application for funds for a special program of services for some 600 adult female prisoners in our state. Let me share with you some cold, hard statistics about these women: 59% had been living in poverty below a minimum standard of living and 81% did not finish high school. Nearly half were functionally illiterate and 588 out of 600 adult female prisoners had at least one child.

Who cares for their children?

At this very time when there is a cry from many to cut taxes, there is a counter cry for more services. A call for national health programs, for decent housing, for jobs, for more prisons, for roads, for airports, for less air and water pollution, and for a better quality of life.

In short, the question is: How does government do more with less?

---

2. Matthew 25:35-36, 40

A governor of one of our states recently said that if individuals are willing to increase their commitment to obligations in such a way as to take care of their families, their neighbors, and their neighbor's neighbors, then government can be seriously contained. But if family fragmentation and community disinterest persist, and individuals do not feel any obligation to the communities where they live, then people will increasingly rely on government.

As you exit from this Oakhurst meeting house today, glance over at our covenant rock. It is a big rock, a strong mighty rock. A granite rock. One of the strongest of rocks. It is our way of saying that:

We are together only to be the church of God in Christ. We are not here by chance, but God through His grace is making of us a fellowship to embody and to express the Spirit of Christ. Or if you please, as expressions of His Spirit, making of us fragile, desert flowers that we in these days might reflect God's love, and through His love bring Hope and Faith, and Love, these three, to our fellow pilgrims and travelers through the coming hours and days that lie ahead.

# Fernwood

After ten years of visiting and working in the North Georgia mountains of Pickens County at a place we call Fernwood, Clarice and I retired, built a home, and moved to there in 1988.

There are thousands of ferns along Sharp Mountain Creek and all on the slopes of the hills and mountains. It's not exactly a wild remote place, but certainly a quiet place and when we bought these eleven-plus acres, it was not readily and easily accessible, especially in wintertime.

We have come to recognize much of the wildlife that inhabits this place: raccoons, opossums, deer, snakes (both poisonous timber rattlers and copperheads, as well as the harmless black snake), rabbits, red-tailed hawks, buzzards, chipmunks, and squirrels. The birds are robins, Pileated Woodpeckers, wrens, Indigo Buntings, bluebirds, Tufted Titmice, Evening and Rose-Breasted Grosbeaks, sparrows, cardinals, phoebes, chickadees, and many others.

For the first few years we lived here, we seldom saw deer. Now we have photos of deer peering in our bedroom windows. We have spotted them over the years grazing like a bunch of cows and seemingly paying us little or no attention. In fact, to protect some of my azaleas, I actually shot one with my pellet gun.

On July 6, 2000, while picking blueberries in the garden I heard something running toward me and shortly a full-antlered buck burst through the hedge and bounded down the bank to within ten feet of me. It was breathing hard and sweating from running. Shortly I heard a dog, hot on the buck's trail. When the dog burst through the hedge, I yelled at it and it turned away off the trail.

Life here at Fernwood is never dull. There's always something to do, something new to explore. It is amazing to note the changes that occur, not only with the change of the seasons – spring, summer, fall, and winter – but also the changes over time. The winter ice storms took out a lot of pine trees that left big open spaces for new trees and undergrowth to spring forth. Lady Slippers were found in places in the past year that were not there before and in other places, the Lady Slippers have "slipped away." Sharp Mountain Creek itself changes from year to year. Here a bank was cut under and there a new sand bar. Dead limbs from trees will dam up a spot and the water finds a new route, either under, over or around the dam.

Of course, our own interference has made big changes from what it was over 30 years ago. The driveway cut is graded, graveled, and paved. I have planted many native azaleas and rhododendrons along the driveway, nursery area, around the house and west of the house. There's an area cleared out for the nursery and another clearing under the power lines for the garden, blueberries, red raspberries, and a fig bush brought up from 1710 Church Street Extension, where Mother and Dad lived. We also brought roses from the back yard of the old store at Kennesaw Mountain and from Clarice's mother's home in Alabama.

We made lots of changes on the north side of Sharp Mountain Creek, but left untouched the property on the other side of the creek. There was an easement road cut in to provide access to the back of the property that my sister Dot Parker and her husband Dip owned on the south side of the creek. Club mosses have now claimed much of that road.

With more time on our hands, Clarice and I devoted our energies to community interests. I volunteered with the Bethany-Salem volunteer fire department, where I served as the public relations officer. I helped with fund raising, went on fire calls to take photos, and wrote up the fire stories for the *Pickens County Progress*. Oh yes, and I got to ride on a fire truck in the Marble Festival parade one year.

I also volunteered with Habitat for Humanity, taking photos of homes under construction and giving progress reports in newspaper articles.

Clarice became involved with the Sharptop Arts Association where she served as president for several years. With grants received from the Georgia Council for the Arts, Clarice worked with art teachers from the local schools to design and produce a county-wide children and youth art exhibit involving more than 600 young artists. The youth art shows became an annual event and have continued since Clarice stepped down as president several years ago.

I became active with the Master Gardeners and the Georgia Native Plant Society. I always enjoy the beauty of the woods and the mountains here.

This photo is of a rhododendron for which I received an award from the Azalea Chapter (Atlanta chapter) of the American Rhododendron Society at one of their flower shows. The award shown in this photo, however, was made for me by my granddaughter Corinne.

One of the many rhododendrons from Fernwood.

Over the years, I have written several articles for the *Pickens County Progress* about native plants that thrive here at Fernwood. Here are two articles I wrote about native azaleas.

## Bush Honeysuckles?

**The Native Azaleas that abound in Pickens County go unnoticed by many residents.**

What exactly is that bush that has a bloom similar to that of a wild honeysuckle vine? There are thousands of them here in our Pickens County mountains. In the deep woods they will have very few or no blooms. On the edge of the woods or along the roadsides they frequently put on a lavish display of white, yellow, red, or gold blooms.

They are so common around these parts that most folks give them only a passing thought as they travel our roads in the spring of the year. However, a traveler through North Georgia over 200 years ago was utterly amazed when he saw a hillside of these bush honeysuckles in full bloom.

This is what he wrote, "...In the cool, sequestered, rockey vales, we behold ... the fiery azalea, flaming on the ascending hills or wavy surface of the gliding brooks. The epithet fiery, I annex to this most celebrated species of azalea, ... its flowers, which are in general of the colour of the finest red lead, orange, and bright gold, as well as yellow and cream colour; these various splendid colours are not only in separate branches on the same plant; and clusters of the blossoms cover the shrubs in such incredible profusion on the hill sides, that suddenly opening to view from dark shades, we are alarmed with the apprehension of the hill being set on fire. This is certainly the most gay and brilliant flowering shrub yet known." From *Bartram's Travels*, by William Bartram, published 1791.

Over the subsequent 200 years, explorers, botanists and professional plant collectors continued to travel these parts to study and collect specimens of our common bush honeysuckle that is now recognized as an azalea, a member of a much larger family of plants including rhododendrons and blueberries, among others.

In 1951 Henry Skinner spent an entire summer traveling the Southeastern U.S. in search of our native azaleas. He describes a visit to Mt. Oglethorpe here in Pickens County where he discovered the same azalea, *Rhododendron calendulaceum* or Flame Azalea, that William Bartram described nearly 200 years earlier.

However, neither Bartram or Skinner traveled over all of Pickens County. We have both the Piedmont Azalea, *R. canescens*, and no doubt, *R. bakeri* or Cumberland Azalea, as well as *R. calendulaceum*.

These deciduous native azaleas are tough plants. They can be found on steep clay banks, in deep woods, along stream banks and they even survive heavy clear-cutting if the roots are not disturbed.

In the last 30 years they have been rediscovered in our state. The Georgia General Assembly has named the native azalea Georgia's official flowering shrub. The Azalea Chapter of the American Rhododendron Society has some 200 members in Georgia and the Georgia Native Plant Society has featured several articles on these beautiful plants in their official quarterly publication.

Members of the Georgia Native Plant Society have rescued hundreds of these fine plants on rescue missions when the owner or developer grants permission to collect plants in areas that are about to be cleared for roads, housing developments, golf courses, or shopping centers.

Most nurseries offer only a limited selection of these plants. Homeplace Gardens at Commerce and Transplant Nursery in Lavonia, GA, formerly offered native azaleas to retail public but are now mostly wholesale. Here in Pickens County, Kinzer Nursery has a large collection of these plants available.

You can grow wild with native azaleas!

By Francis E. Stewart

*Pickens County Progress*, August 28, 2003

## Eye Candy for Dog Days of August

Would you like to have a red flowering native azalea that blooms in the hottest Dog Days of late July and August?

If you wanted one, it may be rather hard to find. It is the Plumleaf Azalea (*Rhododendron prunifolium*), a native shrub of West Central Georgia and East Central Alabama. Callaway Gardens are located in this area and this azalea has been chosen for the Gardens logo. South of the Gardens and near Lumpkin, Georgia, it is blooming in Providence Canyon State Park, one of the hottest spots in Georgia.

It is easy to grow, relatively disease resistant, tolerates full sun, but shows off best in the edge of the woods or along a driveway. It is one of the showiest of the native azaleas. Color may range from reddish orange to red.

We have several blooming now. A few are 12 to 14 feet tall and eight feet wide. We are blessed with a most pleasant distraction from the hot Dog Days. We also enjoy watching the butterflies take their fill of the blooms.

More information about this and other native azaleas can be found in our local library. Look for *Azaleas*, a book by Fred Galle. Also, in a couple of weeks look for the book *American Azaleas* by Clarence Towe.

By Francis E. Stewart

*Pickens County Progress*, August 13, 2009


The *Rhododendron prunifolium* is featured on the cover of this book.

I often write letters to the editor. Below I voiced my feelings as an Advent season approached.

## Christmas Season --
## a poignant time to ponder America's justice system

A recent editorial in the *Progress* seems to me to be quite appropriate to ponder as we enter the Advent season of the year. How is the question, "Do life imprisonment sentences serve justice?" related to "The Season?"

Consider our Master's last hours on the cross and His justice to the criminals, "This day thou shalt be with me in paradise," and secondly, "I was in prison and ye visited me...." "Inasmuch as ye have done it unto the least of these, ye have done it unto me."

Jails, justice, and the entire criminal justice system are, in fact, related to the Christmas season. Yet we forget or prefer to "lock 'em up and throw away the key."

For nearly 40 years I have noted the ebb and flow of Georgia's and the Nation's lawmakers attempts to respond to the voters' conflicting demands for justice. Rehabilitation and restoration to society vs. punishment. ("The more punishment, the better.")

'Ole Lester Maddox is reported to have said, "We will have a better prison system when we get a better grade of prisoners." Hard to fault that statement. However, now the "better grade of prisoners" are assigned to community service, holding a job, staying at home, and looking after the family during the week, but picking up trash on our streets and roadways, painting, repairing, restoring public buildings, and so forth, on weekends.

So what do we do with the teenagers, youth, adults, and older adults who are sent away to Alto and Reidsville diagnostic and classification centers, regional and state Youth Development Centers (now renamed Youth Detention Centers) and the literally dozens of other state and county detention centers and jails around the state?

Boot camps were the way to go a few years back. However, from the reports I received, only about half or less stayed out of trouble with the police and courts after getting out of boot camps.

Now we have lots of new jails around the state and, I understand, still more under construction. Over 50,000 in our jails and many backed up in county jails waiting to be sent to the state system. To save money, the state has even turned over operation of some of the state prisons to private contractors.

However, there remains a big problem: finding the money to hire and pay enough guards and other necessary staff to safely operate and maintain these vast systems. Recent reports indicate many of the state and some of the private jails cannot hire and keep adequate staff.

The vast majority of boys and girls, men and women among the tens of thousands now in our prison system will eventually be released.

The questions are, will they be better or worse from having spent days, months, or years in prison? Have they had opportunities to learn a trade, or for some, learn to read and write while in jail? Will those who are mentally ill receive humane treatment? Will the young, first-time offender be protected from bitter, hardened criminals while in jail? Will the prisoner, male or female, be visited regularly by family members and church-going, God-loving folks in this holiday season and the year and years to come?

By Francis E. Stewart

*Pickens County Progress*, December 2, 1999

## Thoughts on Lent:
## Palm Sunday to Easter, What Happens?

Hope, anger, betrayal, fear, suffering, agape love, triumph, new beginning, new direction. It is difficult to compress all of the fears, changes, and rapidly-changing events compressed into such a few days time.

This weekend Palm Sunday will be celebrated in churches around the world with palm branches, great music, and a retelling of the Story.

The Last Supper, prayer in Gethsemene, and Good Friday will not likely be given more than a few passing moments, yet Good Friday represents the holy supreme message of forgiving love, agape love – self-giving love, love that outlasts time and eternity.

The crass commercialism of Easter holds forth well before Easter Sunday with Easter bunny dolls and candy eggs filling the stores. Dry goods stores hawking spring garments.

Children's Easter egg hunts on the White House lawn and in gardens and pastures across the country. Just as Christmas and Thanksgiving days are commercialized, so is Easter.

Once again, the message of agape love should respond to crass commercialism.

Moreover, the clear call is to be peacemakers, forgiving our enemies. The long, hard road to peace.

Peace within and a continuing year-long witness for peace at home and abroad. Shelter for the homeless, food for the hungry, care for the sick, forgotten, and lonely.

Let agape reign supreme again and again!

Francis E. Stewart, April 2, 2009

Fernwood

Clarice and Francis, May 2011

# Prayer of Gratitude and Hope

O God, thou who stands above and beyond the chaos and the mystery, thou who art also at the very pulsating center of the mystery, in the litter and mulch on the forest floor,

Help us to recognize with deep gratitude, the ten thousand times ten thousand tiny doors of awakening, discovery, learning, and opportunity that silently await our moment of patience and humility and that prepare us for discovery.

Forgive our foolish, destructive pathways that have led us to ever tighter and more restrictive circles of self-seeking, until we are tightly bound in chains of pride and greed, so that we no longer know even ourselves. Strangers we are, because we don't know who we are and what we are capable of becoming and seemingly, no longer care.

Like driven fools, we dash madly to and fro, endlessly chasing bright colored, flashing soap bubbles that as quickly vanish.

Help us to know and feel, if not to see, the hidden hands that stretch across, over, and under the land that gives us life and sustains us. Moreover, help us to know and be more aware of the hidden hands and hearts of gratitude that stretch through the centuries, that provide us with the knowledge and skills we possess in our collective being.

Help us Lord, to give back to them, to one another, and to those who follow us, our gratitude to Thee for allowing us a brief time here on Earth, to contemplate its treasure and mystery.

But above all, help us to so look to Thee, and with such a sense of wonder and gratitude, that others too will stop, look, listen, reflect, and fall on their knees in thanksgiving for creation, Christmas, Good Friday, Easter, and Thy self-giving love to all of us.

There is indeed the Everlasting here in us and on this planet Earth and amidst the cosmic order, of which we are only now beginning to see dimly, as a dark forest that begins to stir as life senses the awakening dawn.

Amen and Amen.

# Benediction

Oh Lord, Our Lord, how excellent is thy name in all the earth.

Even before the mountains were brought forth and from everlasting to everlasting, Thou art God!

Help us to be mindful of Thy loving kindness and of the needs of others as we go forth and into the next days.

May thy spirit uplift us and guide us. May thy spirit direct us in the pathways of service to Thee and to our fellow man.

May the grace and peace of God the Father, the Son, and the Holy Spirit be in and abide with us, now and always.

In the spirit of the Master, we pray.

Amen.

# Acknowledgements

My life has been both enriched and sustained by a vast network of family members, friends, and colleagues. Childhood years on the farm, learning the value of hard work. Doing chores: milking cows, feeding livestock, and cleaning out barns and chicken houses.

Grandmother Minnie Pritchard who spent time with her grandchildren in her garden. Oppedal, O'Neal, and Capener cousins who were my childhood playmates.

My mother, Grace Pritchard Stewart, who even after a very hard day helping Dad with harvest and preparing our evening supper, found time to read to us and opened my door for a lifetime of learning.

Fellow pastors who have been close friends over the years, George McMaster, Lee Wilson, Burch Fannin, George Fields, Jim Prevatt, Heslip "Happy" Lee, and more recently, J. Andrew Lipscomb and rediscovered old friend Irvin Cheney.

My children Frank, Donna, and Susan and grandchildren Jeanne and Corinne, whom I'm proud to say are all contributing members of society and gainfully employed.

Donna, without whose skills in writing, editing, and layout, this book would not have been completed. Reba Shoulders, Mary Margaret (Sandy) Jordan, and Mary Julia Orr who assisted with proof-reading and editing.

Cover photo of *Rhododendron prunifolium* was taken by Al Cook of Pittsboro, NC, the husband of my niece, Daphne Hill. Thank you, Al for this beautiful photo. Cover photo of cornfield and back cover photo were taken by Donna Born.

Articles from the *Pickens County Progress* and letters to the editor are reprinted here with permission. My appreciation to Dan Pool, Editor, *Pickens County Progress*.

www.ingramcontent.com/pod-product-compliance
Lightning Source LLC
Chambersburg PA
CBHW060824050426
42453CB00008B/585